# Travelling the Highway
# My Way of Life

Anthony Cooke

**TRICORN**
**BOOKS**

www.tricornbooks.co.uk

Travelling the Highway
My Way of Life
Anthony Cooke

Design © 131 Design Ltd
www.131design.org
Text © Anthony Cooke

ISBN 978-0-9573435-1-1

A CIP catalogue record for this book is available from the British Library.

Published 2012 by Tricorn Books,
a trading name of 131 Design Ltd.
131 High Street, Old Portsmouth,
PO1 2HW

www.tricornbooks.co.uk

*Front cover pictures*:
Portsmouth City Bus & a local Tour Coach, reproduced with kind permission from Vision Travel.

Printed & bound in Portsmouth by Bishops Printers Ltd

# Contents

# Introduction

# MY STORY

Welcome to my book

## *Travelling the Highway*
## *My Way of Life*

An illustrated account of my travel experiences and places visited over the past years as a P.C.V. driver in Portsmouth area.

P.C.V. Drivers Licence.

Driver C.P.C course was taken with Zenith Driver training of Lee on Solent, Hampshire, in March 2011, as required.

The Certificate of Professional Competence is not a driving licence and mine expires 2019.

# PORTSMOUTH & SOUTHSEA
## Departure points

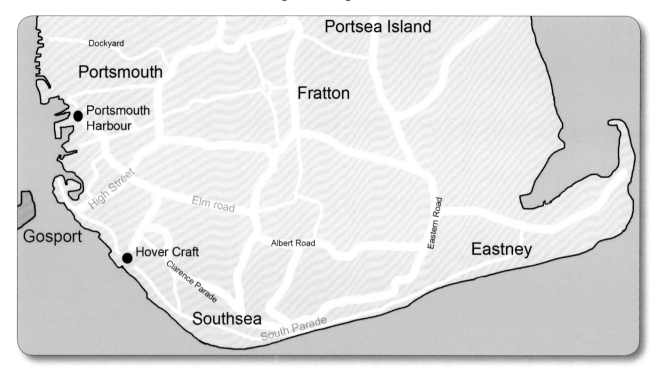

# PORTSMOUTH
## Departure points for all European destinations,
## as detailed on this European Map

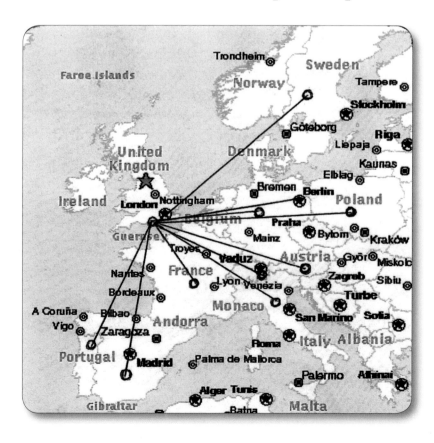

Passenger Transport
from the early days

Change for the
bus industry
in the
Portsmouth area

### City of Portsmouth
Passenger Transport Department

## 75 YEARS
## OF MUNICIPAL TRANSPORT

**First Electric Tram Route**
**Inaugurated 24th September 1901**

City of Portsmouth Passenger Transport Department
Highland Road
Southsea Hants
PO4 9HE

City of Portsmouth Passenger Transport Department

75th Anniversary

1901 — 1976

CITY OF PORTSMOUTH PASSENGER TRANSPORT DEPARTMENT

1901 — 1976

75th ANNIVERSARY

Special Commemorative Envelope issued on 24 September 1976
to mark the inauguration of the first electric Tram Route in
Portsmouth on 24 September 1901.

The special handstamp depicts the Leyland National Bus — one of
Portsmouth's newest buses.

Envelope and Handstamp designed by the Department and produced
by the Portsmouth City Council Printing Service.

**Portsmouth
City Transport**

Safe Driving awards for 1989 and 1990

# Southdown Portsmouth

## Vehicle registration

VWT 618

UWP 105

JPU 817

NFX 667

YDG 616

WVT 618

WAD 644Y

B277 RHC

A474 NJK

A475 NJK

A476 NJK

A477 NJk

C473 CAP

C474 CAP

404DCD

408DCD

412DCD

413DCD

414DCD

416DCD

418DCD

419DCD

423DCD

## Services from Portsmouth

075 London Victoria Coach Station

065 Via Brighton

626 Swansea

# Southdown buy-out

LEWES-BASED NBC subsidiary Southdown Motor Services has now been officially bought by its present senior management.All employees will be given the chance to acquire shares in the company. Southdown, the 47th subsidiary to be sold by NBC since the privatisation programme began 15 months ago, employs about 800 staff and 320 buses, minibuses & coaches on services throughout Sussex & East Hampshire. Its coaches are also used on excursions & tours in many parts of Britain & Europe. Founded in 1915, Southdown was part of British Electric Traction (BET) Group before coming into state owership shortly before the formation of National Bus Company in 1969. Under NBC Southdown was also given control of Brighton Hove and District Omnibus Co. Ltd. This arrangement lasted until January 1986 when the two operations were again seperated prior to privatisation.

# Portsmouth Transit

Red Admiral                                                            Blue Admiral

Portsmouth Transit Ltd   259 Highland Road, Southsea
P04 9HE   Tel 0705 815452   Fax 0705 830230

# NEW ADMIRAL IN PORTSMOUTH

A large part of Stagecoach's Southdown Portsmouth operation was acquired by the Transit Holding Group on Sunday 20th January 1991.

## Red Admiral and Blue Admiral

Operations in Portsmouth will be devided into two; Red Admiral covering the old Southdown routes to Fareham, Waterlooville and Petersfield. Blue Admiral for the old Portsmouth Corporation services on Portsea Island and Paulsgrove.

Red Admiral and Blue Admiral will be seperate limited companies but in every other respect the new companies will reflect the Transit Holding belief in small operational units and short lines of communication.

# Portsmouth Transit

## Vehicle registration

C472CAP

C473 CAP

C474CAP

WOA644Y

B277 RHC

422 DCD

A474NJK

A475 NJK

A476 NlK

A477 NlK

## Services from Portsmouth

075 London Victoria Coach Station

300 BRISTOL

626 Swansea

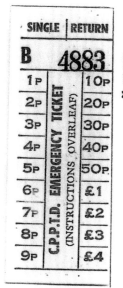

| SINGLE | RETURN |
|---|---|
| **B 4883** | |
| 1P | 10P |
| 2P | 20P |
| 3P | 30P |
| 4P | 40P |
| 5P | 50P |
| 6P | £1 |
| 7P | £2 |
| 8P | £3 |
| 9P | £4 |

C.P.P.T.D. EMERGENCY TICKET (INSTRUCTIONS OVERLEAF)

**Portsmouth Transit**
Red Admiral          Blue Admiral
259 Highland Road • Southsea • PO4 9HE • Tel: 0705 815452
Fax: 0705 830230

23 January 1991

As you know, the Transit Holdings Group has acquired a significant part of the former Portsmouth Citybus and Southdown operations from Sunday 20 January 1991.

Initially, the company will run as Portsmouth Transit Limited from the City Council's former Bus Depot at Eastney. However, in due course it will be split into two companies; Blue Admiral for those services historically provided by CPPTD and Red Admiral for the former Southdown routes.

**PORTSMOUTH RED-RIDER**

B004783

**ALL ROUTE TRAVEL**

ON PCB & RED ADMIRAL
BUS SERVICES

**ONE WEEK**

**Portsmouth:** Red Admiral rider ticket
for one week.

When deregulation came into force People's Provincial moved into Portsmouth with their stage carriage services.

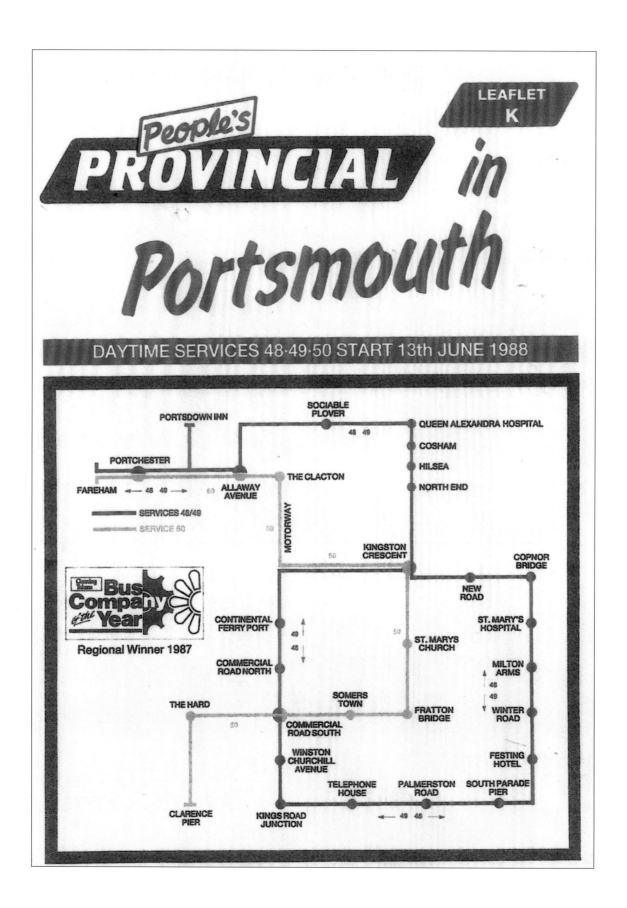

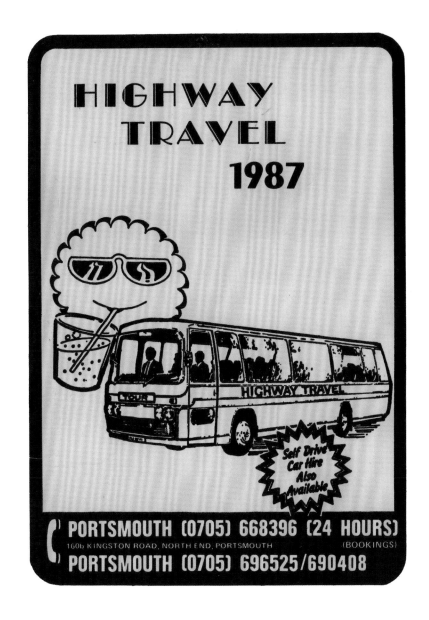

Highway Travel coach tub 25m parked at Little Whitehouse filling station, Newport, Isle of Wight.

# HIGHWAY TRAVEL 1987

## BRUSSELS – COLOGNE AND THE RHINE VALLEY

**5 days – 3 nights**

This tour again packs so much in such a short space of time, but at a leisurely pace – we want you to be awake and fresh to enjoy the delights of such cities as Brussels and Cologne, and the breathtaking beauty of the River Rhine.

DAY 1. This afternoon your HIGHWAY TRAVEL coach will whisk you away from Portsmouth area to Sheerness for an overnight sailing to Flushing on which a Pullman seat has been reserved for you.

DAY 2. Docking early morning, you will be taken through Belgium and on to Germany, crossing the border at Aachen. You are scheduled to arrive at your hotel in Cologne late afternoon. The evening will be free for you to enjoy the delights of the city as you will.

DAY 3. Leaving Cologne after breakfast we will travel down the Rhine Valley, first reaching Bonn, the capital of West Germany– "Beethoven's City". Passing through this university city, we head south to Koblenz, where the Rhine and Mosel rivers meet. As you move down the Rhine, romance begins to fill the air, as castles and fortresses take over from offices and factories. The coach will stop at Rudesheim, where a cruise back up the river is recommended, meeting the coach again at Boppard. During the cruise, enjoy the fairy-tale beauty of this part of the Rhine, with such sights as Goarhousen and the Loreley Rock. From Boppard it's back to Cologne for your overnight stay.

DAY 4. After breakfast we depart for a leisurely drive back to Antwerp via the city of Brussels, where you will be given a short tour of the city seeing the King's Palace, Place Royals, the Church of Notre Dame and the Palais d'Egmont where the U.K. signed to join the E.E.C. On to Antwerp for an overnight stay.

DAY 5. After breakfast it's back to Flusing for a midday sailing to Sheerness. Arriving back in the Portsmouth area late evening.

Departure Dates: 2nd May  23rd May
                 11th July  15th August
COST:            Adults £98.00  Child £88.50
                 *Single Room Supplement:* £18.00
PRICE INCLUDES:  Coach fare throughout, including tours
                 Bed and breakfast with private facilities
                 Return ferry fares

# DORSET TRAVEL SERVICES

Dorset Travel Services Ltd.,
Transport Depot,
Mallard Road,
Bournemouth,
Dorset. BH8 9PN.

Mr T Cook
c/o National Express Inspectors
Portsmouth Travel Interchange

Telephone: 0202 537568 (Depot)
0929 554588 (Office)

18 April 1991
PD SK

Dear Mr Cook

With reference to your recent interview held in Portsmouth, I am pleased to confirm your engagement as a PSV driver with this company based at Portsmouth. The conditions of employment etc., are as discussed with you at the interview.

Our operations in Portsmouth commence on Sunday 21 April 1991 and rosters and duties are being prepared and will be available for collection on Saturday 20 April.

I look forward to a harmonious working relationship which is very essential for our company and I would like to reiterate the points raised during the interview where the most important consideration of your employment is reliability, honesty, driving with due care and consideration for all other road users and respect for the passengers which we carry, treating them in a way in which you would like to be treated yourself. Also when instructed by supervisors of various authorities, acting on their instructions to maintain the agreeable relationship that this company has built up and is determined to continue.

I thank you for your co-operation and assistance in what is so dependable to our future and look forward to having you join our 'team'.

Yours sincerely

# DORSET TRAVEL (EXPRESS) SERVICES

## Services from Portsmouth

075 London Victoria Coach Station

074

072 Via Southampton

065 Via Worthing

300 Bristol

303 Southport

310 Bradford

315 Plymouth

333 Bristol to Blackpool

Start of the 075 to London: Victoria Coach Station

Driver: A.E. Cooke

## COACH REGISTRATIONS

| | | | | |
|---|---|---|---|---|
| B454AAT | G342FFX | G341FFX | G343FFX | D24NWO |
| H352 MLJ | A908LWU | H353 MLJ | H351 MLJ | G345FFX |
| G422FFX | A909LWU | A907LWU | C302 PPE | B554AAT |
| H348JFX | C203 PPE | J40 DTS | H346JFX | H339 KPR |
| H818AHS | G341 FFS | H815AHS | PJI3354 | H371 VCG |
| G344FFX | H374 JFX | H343 MLJ | H349ML | G327 PEW |
| H352 MLJ | K354VRU | G328 PEW | K355VRU | LDZ2948 |
| L331 BFX | G329 PEW | K594VBC | H326DTR | K595VBC |
| L332 BFX | L132 BFX | K334VRU | M359LFX | M356LFX |
| M358LFX | M326LFX | M360LFX | M357LFX | H338KPR |
| H339KPR | N369TJT | M365LFX | M357LFY | N370TJT |
| N3901JT | | | | |

Febuary 9th 1998
Cardiff to Little Canada, Isle of Wight
Activity Centre – Coach M214 UYD

View of Fishbourne Ferry Port, Isle of Wight

Arrived Barcelona. Coach parked up

# TRAVEL DETAILS

## OUTWARD TRAVEL

**14/02/98**

| | |
|---|---|
| 14H00 | Coach to meet party at school to load luggage. |
| 14H30 | Coach to depart school. |
| 16H00 | Check-in at P&O car ferry terminal, Dover (1 hour prior to departure). |
| 17H00 | Depart Dover. |
| 20H15 | Arrive Calais, local time. |
| | Proceed to Barcelona. |
| **15/02/98** 15H30 | Arrive Hotel Ronda (approximately) for evening dinner, first included meal |

## HOMEWARD TRAVEL

**19/02/98**

| | |
|---|---|
| 16H00 | Coach to depart Hotel Ronda |
| **20/02/98** 11H15 | Check-in at P&O car ferry terminal, Calais (1 hour prior to departure). |
| 12H15 | Depart Calais |
| 12H30 | Arrive Dover (local time) |
| | Proceed to Ellen Wilkinson School |
| 15H00 | Arrive school (approximately) |

Bull Ring, Barcelona

15

## Coach Operator:

Priory Coaches of GOSPORT
Quay Lane
Hardway
Gosport
Hants
PO12 4LJ

Tel: (01705) 580527

## EXCURSION DETAILS

16.02.98

Depart the hotel after breakfast for a morning visit to the wine producer Torres, this has been pre-booked for your group:

**Torres - Wine producer**
**Comercio 22,**
**08720 - Vilafranca del Penedes**
**(Barcelona)**
**Spain**
**Tel: 0034 3 817 7400 From the UK**
**Time: 10.30**
**Cost: Free**

Rest of the day at leisure. Sightseeing enroute back to the hotel for dinner.

**17.02.98**

Group to organise this day in resort, please consult the tour driver the previous night.

**18.02.98**

Morning visit to the Gas Natural site, has been pre-booked for your group:

**Gas Natural**
**Avda. Porta de l'Angel, 22**
**Tel: 0034 3 402 51 00 from the UK**
**Time: 10.00**
**Cost: Free**

Rest of the day at lesiure. Please liaise closely with the tour driver as to requirements.

**NB: Please note that on executive express tours involving overnight travel on the coach, use of the coach and drivers is not permitted upon arrival on day 2 and prior to departure on the penultimate day.**

May 3rd 1998 — Alton Towers

Coach D/D; C381 NHJ and J461 JRV

July 1998 - Lido Di Jesolo (Venezia) Italy
Tour Coach K807 EET


Laguna di Venezia

July 1998 Tour of Italy (Venice)

September 20th 1998 (Narrow entrance)
Outdoor Sculpture Museum nr Salisbury
Coach M214 UYD

September 20th 1998 Roche Court Sculpture Park

Back Flip sculpture (£75,000 + vat)

## Saturday 13 February 1999

The group will be met at school by their coach at 06:30 hrs to load luggage ready for departure by 07:00 hrs. We would suggest that the group take provisions from home for the journey and suitable stops will be made en route as necessary.

The group will continue their journey and upon arrival into York, the group will be transferred as near as possible to **York Minster**, where it is intended that the group conduct a self-guided tour at 15.00 hrs.

Following the above, the group will board their coach and continue to their accommodation which has been arranged at the   New Racecourse Centre.

Arrival is anticipated at approximately 17:00 hrs. Here, the group will spend the next 2 nights with Full Board commencing with dinner this evening.

After dinner, the coach will be required to transfer the group to/from Clifford's Tower, where arrangements have been made for the group to undertake the **Original Ghost Walk of York**. The walk will commence at 20.00 hrs and will end at approximately 21.30 hrs. The group will then require the coach to transfer back to the Centre.

**PLEASE LIAISE CLOSELY WITH YOUR DRIVER REGARDING ANY TRANSFERS OR PICKUPS YOU MAY REQUIRE DURING THE TOUR. PLEASE ALSO REMEMBER THAT YOUR TOUR MUST COMPLY WITH DRIVER'S HOURS' REGULATIONS AND THAT YOUR DRIVER'S DECISION IS FINAL.**

**PLEASE ALSO NOTE THAT ROOMS IF PREVIOUSLY OCCUPIED, MAY NOT BE AVAILABLE UNTIL MID/LATE-AFTERNOON.**

**PLEASE REMEMBER TO TAKE TOWELS AND TOILETRIES FROM HOME AS THESE ARE NOT GENERALLY PROVIDED.**

## Sunday 14 February 1999

This morning, the group will into the City centre and proceed firstly to the **Jorvik Viking Centre**, Coppergate, where admission will be in 2 smaller parties. Group 1 will be admitted at 10.00 hrs, followed by Group 2 at 10.15 hrs.

The group will then proceed to the **Castle Museum** for 12.00 hrs, where a booking has been arranged by NST.

Following the above, the group will continue to the **Yorkshire Museum,** Museum Gardens - where arrival is expected at 15.00 hrs.

The group will return to the Racecourse Centre in time for dinner. They will then depart by coach for the **York Megabowl,** Clifton Moor Retail Park, where 1 game of bowling has been arranged for 19.30 hrs. Return to the Centre by coach.

## Monday 15 February 1999

The group will vacate their rooms after breakfast and load luggage on to the coach ready for departure on the homeward journey later this morning. Packed lunches will be provided on departure (last meal included in the tour cost)

Opportunity for the group to see the City Walls & famous 'Bars' before continuing to the **York Story**, St Mary's, Castlegate. Here, a booking has been made on behalf of the group and admission is arranged for 10.00 hrs.

At 11.00 hrs, the homeward journey will continue and arrival back at school is anticipated at approximately 18:00 hrs.

April 4th 1999 Trip to Claviere, Italy


On arrival at Claviere (coach broke down)
Reg R204 WYD towed to Milan for repair

# ITALY

COACH OPERATOR:

PRIORY COACHES OF GOSPORT
QUAY lANE
HARDWAY;
COS PORT
HANTS
P012 4LJ
TEL: (01705) 580522

24 hour eniergency telephone no: (01705) 580522

CROSS CHANNEL COMPANY:

P & 0 STENA LINE
CHANNEL HOUSE
CHANNEL VIEW ROAD
DOVER. KENT
CT17 9TJ
TEL 01304 203388

Montecantini
Coach S749 XYA

# TRAVEL DETAILS

## OUTWARD TRAVEL

**FRIDAY 9TH JULY 1999**

| | |
|---|---|
| 15H30 | Coach to meet party at school to load luggage. |
| 15H45 | Coach to depart school. |
| 18H45 | Check-in at P & O Stena car ferry terminal, Dover (1 hour prior to departure). |
| 19H45 | Depart Dover |
| 22H00 | Arrive Calais (local time). |
| | Proceed to Montecatini |

**SATURDAY 10TH JULY 1999**

| | |
|---|---|
| 19H00 | Arrive Hotel Splendid (approximately). First included meal will be evening meal |

## HOMEWARD TRAVEL

**WEDNESDAY 14TH JULY 1999**

| | |
|---|---|
| | Party to vacate rooms after breakfast and load luggage onto coach. |
| 16H45 | Coach to depart Hotel Splendid and travel overnight to Calais. |

**THURSDAY 15TH JULY 1999**

| | |
|---|---|
| 13H45 | Check-in at P & O Stena Line car ferry terminal, Calais (1 hour prior to departure). |
| 14H45 | Depart Calais. |
| 15H00 | Arrive Dover (local time). |
| | Proceed to college. |
| 18H00 | Arrive college (approximately). |

Leaning Tower of Pisa, Italy

# EXCURSION DETAILS

SATURDAY 10TH - WEDNESDAY 14TH JULY 1999
PLEASE SEE ATTACHED INFORMATION FROM GROUP AS TO PROPOSED ITINERARY.

SUNDAY 11TH JULY, 1999
Guide to meet group at 11h00 for 3 hours tour in Siena at the bus parking area in Via Veneto
PAOLO FALDONI - TEL: 0337 977830

MONDAY 12TH JULY, 1999
Guide to meet group at 10h00 for 3 hours tour in Florence at the parking area located at the
Fortezza da Basso
CHIARA MIGLIORINI - TEL: 055 644681 or 0337 958521

**ASK THE HOTEL MANAGER/RECEPTION STAFF TO CALL THE GUIDES THE DAY
PRIOR TO THE GUIDED TOUR TO ENSURE ALL IS IN ORDER AND THERE HAVE BEEN
NO LAST MINUTE CHANGES.**

**Group can use the coach for any excursion requirements subject to EC regulations
governing driver hours.**

Please note that on executive express tours involving overnight travel on the coach, use of the
coach and drivers is not permitted upon arrival on day 2 and prior to departure on the
penultimate day.

-------------------------------

**Generous travel timings to and from port are normally set by the coach company,
taking into account the possibility of any delays. Should this result in a port arrival
well ahead of schedule, your group may travel on an earlier ferry crossing, subject to
availability.**

-------------------------------

We would strongly advise you of the need to observe the unloading of suitcases from the
coach and safe transportation of **each** case into the hotel on arrival.

We have had several recent instances of opportunist theft of suitcases from city coach tours
and we feel we should point this out to groups to avoid the obvious serious inconvenience and
distress this causes.

We recommend the same procedure is followed when loading suitcases for the return journey.

-------------------------------

November 3rd 1999, German Exchange border
Coach R636 VYB

The Berlin Wall

**Saturday 10th July**
Arrive lunchtime in Montecantini. Afternoon free for students to spend in Montecantini.

**Sunday 11th July**
Coach travel to Sienna (1 hour approx.). Three hour guided tour of Sienna starting at 11am, afternoon to explore. Leave at approximately 16h00.

**Monday 12th July**
Full day in Florence (30 minute coach trip). Three hour guided tour in the morning starting at 10am, followed by some personal sight seeing time. Return to hotel early evening (17h00) for dinner.

**Tuesday 13th July**
Morning trip to Florence leaving at 09h00. In the afternoon (13h00), transfer to Pisa to see the leaning tower. Evening return (16h00) to Montecantini.

**Wednesday 14th July**
Morning free, return home in afternoon.

November 3rd 1999  A house in Postdam

Year 2000 'Priory Garage' Gosport

# CORBU TRIP 1999

**DAY ONE**
Thursday Nov.11th.

Leave Portsmouth Guildhall **12.01am.**
Travel by coach to **LA TOURETTE** arrive
1530 approx.
1930 (prompt) Supper
2030 Meet in Chapter House

**DAY TWO**
Friday Nov.12

0730-0900 Self-Serve Breakfast
**0900 LA TOURETTE TOUR**
**1230 LUNCH AT LA TOURETTE**
Afternoon to **LYON** visit
(Calatrava,Botta,Piano,School of Achitecture etc)
To Centre of Lyon for evening
Return late to spend night at **LA TOURETTE**

**DAY THREE**
Saturday Nov.13

Pack up rooms and bags to coach **before**
O730 Breakfast
0800 (prompt) leave La Tourette
Travel by coach to **RONCHAMP** arrive 1300
approx. Picnic Lunch. Vist. Leave 1500.

and stay the night at Arc et Senans.

**DAY FOUR**
Sunday Nov.14

0800 Breakfast
0900 Tour of Arc et Senans
1000 leave travel home via ferry from
Calais to Dover.
Arrive Portsmouth early evening.

**JMP & TW   09.11.'99**

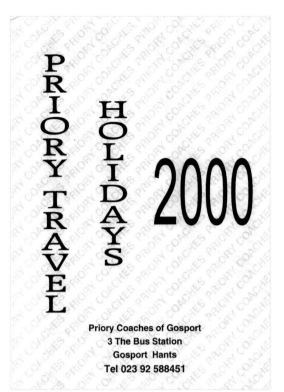

## PRIORY TRAVEL HOLIDAYS 2000

**Priory Coaches of Gosport**
3 The Bus Station
Gosport Hants
Tel 023 92 588451

## GERMAN CHRISTMAS MARKETS £155
### COLOGNE & DUSSELDORF

## EDINBURGH TATTOO & THE ROYAL YACHT BRITANNIA £189

THIS FOUR DAY BREAK INCLUDES NOT ONLY
A TOP PRICE TICKET TO THE WORLD
RENOWNED EDINBURGH MILITARY TATTOO,
BUT ALSO A VISIT TO THE ROYAL YACHT
BRITANNIA. A PACKED PROGRAMME FULL OF
POMP & CEREMONY........
**SUN 20th - WED 23rd AUG**

> **The Thistle Hotel Irvine** is on the Firth of Clyde, 10 miles
> from Glasgow. Each room has been refurbished and offers
> tea / coffee tray. The hotel has a Hawaii Lagoon fun pool
> and jacuzzi.

## BERLIN AND POTSDAM £359

TRAVEL AND ACCOMMODATION DETAILS

SATURDAY 25 MARCH 2000

The coach will arrive at school half an hour before the scheduled departure time. Please ensure that all members of staff are carrying their passports with them on their person as these will be checked prior to crossing the channel.

Please ensure that you have filled in the enclosed P&O Passenger Registration Form and that you have it ready to hand to your coach driver who will in turn hand it in at Dover Port.

COACH OPERATED BY: PRIORY COACHES EMERGENCY TEL: 01705-580522.

| | | | |
|---|---|---|---|
| DEPART | : SCHOOL | | AT 17:00 |
| ARRIVE | : DOVER EASTERN DOCK | | AT 19:30 |
| | | | |
| DEPART | : DOVER EASTERN DOCK | (P & O EUROPEAN FERRIES Ref: f20366250) | AT 20:30 |
| ARRIVE | : CALAIS | | AT 22:45 |
| | | | |
| DEPART | : CALAIS | | AT 23:00 |
| ARRIVE | : HOTEL SPAIN | 26 MARCH | AT 16:00 |

SUNDAY 26 MARCH 2000

Arrive at your hotel and check-in.

Evening meal at your hotel. Please reconfirm exact meal timings with your hotelier on arrival.

Evening at leisure (please note that the coach will not be available for use on this evening

| | | |
|---|---|---|
| HOTEL | : Carlos 1 | Full Board for 4 nights |
| ADDRESS | : Ronda Sant Elm. 4 | 24 Multi-Bedded |
| | : 08360 | 3 Adults |
| | : CANET DE MAR. BARCELONA | 2 Drivers |
| | : SPAIN | |
| TELEPHONE | : 0034(3 7940257 | |

MONDAY 27 MARCH 2000

Breakfast at hotel. Collect packed lunches

Full day excursion to Barcelona

10:00 Visit to Camp Nou. Although there will be no matches on this day you will be able to visit the stadium and the Museu del Futbol Club Barcelona. The price for the two non-guided visits is 325 Ptas, there is no charge for the accompanying adults

Visit to Poble Espanol, for a non-guided visit, the price is 525 Ptas per person
Marques de Comillas, s/n
Tel: 0034 93325 7866

Packed lunch

For a visit to the Estadi Olympic, a reservation is possible at 17:30 although we appreciate that this may be too late for you. Unfortunately this time is the only one available. However, entry to the stadium for a NON-GUIDED visit is free of charge. We are confirming that this is the case as if so, it will give you more flexibility to do this visit on the day. *MONDAY*

Please liaise with your drivers as to where and when to meet you. The coach can transport the group to the Placa de Armada where you can take the Transbordador Aereo across the harbour to Barceloneta. The price for one way travel only is 800 Ptas per person.

Please liaise with your drivers as to where and when you would like to be picked up to begin your return journey back to the hotel

Evening meal at the hotel

## TUESDAY 28 MARCH 2000

Breakfast at hotel. Collect packed lunches

Visit to Figueres

Visit to the Museu Dali, you have a reservation for 10:30. The price is 800 Ptas per person

Visit to Cadaques

Packed lunch

Early evening at leisure (possible visit to Empuries)
Return to the hotel for the evening meal

## WEDNESDAY 29 MARCH 2000

Breakfast at hotel. Collect packed lunches

Full day excursion to Barcelona

Visit to the Sagrada Familia
Mallorca, 401 (08013)
Tel: 0034 93 455 02 47

Walk along Las Ramblas, this unique, lively and colourful boulevard runs from the Placa de Cataluyna down to the port

Visit to Barcelona's Gothic Quarter

Return to the hotel for the evening meal

## THURSDAY 30 MARCH 2000

```
Breakfast at hotel. Collect packed lunches
Please ensure that all rooms are vacated at specified time
and that all personal belongings are removed.

Morning and afternoon at leisure


Depart   : resort                        At 17:00

Arrive   : Calais            31 March  At 10:00


Friday 31 march 2000

Depart:Calais (P&O European Ferries ref: f20366250)At 11:00
Arrive : Dover Eastern Dock                    At 11:15

Depart : Dover Eastern Dock                    At 11:30
Arrive : School                                At 14:00
```

March 2000 Barcelona

Coach R636 VYB

TRAVEL AND ACCOMMODATION DETAILS

TUESDAY 19 SEPTEMBER 2000

DEPART    : SCHOOL                                                        AT 13:45
ARRIVE    : DOVER EASTERN DOCK                                            AT 15:45


DEPART    : DOVER EASTERN DOCK    (P & O EUROPEAN FERRIES Ref: P20362745)  AT 16:45
ARRIVE    : CALAIS                                                         AT 19:00


DEPART    : CALAIS                                                         AT 19:15
ARRIVE    : HOTEL - FRANCE                          20 SEPTEMBER AT 08:30


WEDNESDAY 20 SEPTEMBER 2000

Arrive at your hotel and check-in. Please note that your first included
meal is breakfast at the hotel.

Your coach will not be available for use on this day due to EU Drivers'
Hours regulations.

HOTEL       Hotel Climat De France         Half Board for 5 nights
ADDRESS     Avenue De L'Arc De Triomphe    1 See Main Booking
            84100 ORANGE
TELEPHONE   00 33 4 90 51 8787


Time at leisure in Orange.

Return to your hotel for your evening meal. Please reconfirm your meal
times with your hotelier upon your arrival.

Evening for follow up language work. A room has been requested at your
hotel, please also reconfirm this in advance.

THURSDAY 21 SEPTEMBER 2000

Breakfast at your hotel.

A.M. Visit to Les Baux
You have a booking to visit the Chateau des Baux at 11:30  This includes
a guided tour in French, and costs 18 Francs per child. There is a 1:10
free place ratio for your accompanying staff, with remaining adults
paying 25 Francs.
Please note that in addition to this, the guide will cost 350 Francs.
Please present the Equity voucher upon your arrival.

Contact telephone number : 04 90 54 37 37.

P.M. Visit to the town of Arles on the Van Gogh trail
You have a guided tour of Arles (in French) booked for 15:00. This costs

Evening meal at your hotel followed by language follow-up work.

FRIDAY 22 SEPTEMBER 2000

Breakfast at your hotel.

A.M. Visit to the town of
Entrance to the Roman amphitheatre costs 150 Francs for your group.

P.M. Visit to the Camargue and the town of Aigues-Mortes. Please liaise
with your coach drivers reagrding the exact route and timings should you
have any preferences.

Return to your hotel to freshen up.

Evening meal at your hotel followed by follow-up language work.

SATURDAY 23 SEPTEMBER 2000

Breakfast at your hotel.

A.M. Visit to the Auchan hypermarket complex at Avignon-Sud

P.M. Visit to the Palais des Papes in Avignon.
This has been booked for you for 14 and includes a guided tour in
French. The cost of the visit is 32 Francs for children, with one of
your staff having to pay 36 Francs as well. The other members of staff
gain free entrance.
Telephone : 04 90 27 50 73.

Return to your hotel to freshen up.

Evening meal at your hotel followed by time at leisure.

SUNDAY 24 SEPTEMBER 2000

Breakfast at your hotel.

A.M. Visit to the Pont du Gard

P.M. Visit to the Haribo sweet factory and museum in Uzes
You have a booking for this visit for 14. The cost of this is 15
Francs per child with free places for your accompanying staff.
Telephone : 04 66 22 74 39.

Return to your hotel to freshen up.

Evening meal at your hotel followed by time at leisure.

MONDAY 25 SEPTEMBER 2000

Breakfast at your hotel.

A.M. Time at leisure with possible language work in Orange.

P.M. Start your journey back to Calais and the UK, with a stop-off en
route at the Grottes de la Madeleine.

Please liaise with your coach drivers regarding the exact timings for

this day.

| | | | |
|---|---|---|---|
| DEPART | : HOTEL - FRANCE | | AT 14:00 |
| ARRIVE | : CALAIS | 26 SEPTEMBER | AT 05:15 |

TUESDAY 26 SEPTEMBER 2000

| | | | |
|---|---|---|---|
| DEPART | : CALAIS | (P & O EUROPEAN FERRIES Ref: P20362745) | AT 06:15 |
| ARRIVE | : DOVER EASTERN DOCK | | AT 06:30 |

| | | |
|---|---|---|
| DEPART | : DOVER EASTERN DOCK | AT 06:30 |
| ARRIVE | : SCHOOL | AT 08:15 |

Take a ferry from Venice ( St Marks) for Punta Sabbione where a coach will be waiting for you to tansfer your group to your hotel.

Ferry and coach pick up times will be comfirmed whilst you are in resort.

20:00 Evening meal at your hotel.

Monday 23 October 2000

Breakfast at your hotel. Collect packed lunches

10:30 - 12:00 Rugby Training at Jesolo's rugby grounds.

A coach will transfer your group to and from the grounds.

Afternoon at leisure.

Evening meal at your hotel.

Tenpin bowling at a local bowling rink.

Tuesday 24 October 2000

Breakfast at your hotel

Morning at leisure

Return to your hotel hot lunch.Collect packed dinners

13:30 Depart your hotel

15:00 Civic Reception

18:00 Match against A. Milani in Rovigo

Wednesday 25 October 2000

Breakfasr at your hotel

 Morning at leisure

Return to your hotel for a hot lunch. Collect packed lunches.

14:30 Depart from your hotel for Mirano.

17:00 Match against Mirano Rugby Club

After your match you will be departing for the UK

## TRAVEL AND ACCOMODATION DETAILS

FRIDAY 20 OCTOBER 2000

COACH OPERATED BY: PRIORY COACHES EMERGENCY TEL:02392-580522

| | | |
|---|---|---|
| DEPART : SCHOOL | AT | 15:45 |
| ARRIVE : DOVER | AT | 18:45 |

DEPART : DOVER EASTERN DOCK     ( P&O EUROPEAN FERRIES REF:p2041150) 19:45

| | | |
|---|---|---|
| ARRIVE : CALAIS | AT | 22:00 |
| DEPART : CALAIS | AT | 22:15 |
| ARRIVE : LIDO DI JESOLO     21ST OCTOBER | AT | 17:15 |

SATURDAY 21 OCTOBER 2000

HOTEL  :  Hotel Apollo                    Full Board for 4 nights

Address : Via Colleoni 3                   24 Multi-Bedded

           : LIDO di Jesolo               3 Adults

TELEPHONE  :0039 0421 93317             2 Drivers

Arrive at your hotel and check in

Evening meal at your hotel

Evening at leisure

Evening activities will be confirmed whilst you are in resort and will be organised by your Equity representative.

Sunday 22 October 2000

Breakfast at your hotel . collect packed lunches.

10:30 - 12:00 Rugby Training at Jesolo's rugby grounds.

A coach will transfer your group to the rugby grounds and after the training you will be transfered to Punta Sabbione where you will take a public ferry to Venice ( St Marks).

Day in Venice

DEPART : LIDO DI JESOLO                                          AT 20:30

ARRIVE :CALAIS                              26TH OCTOBER          AT  15:30

TUESDAY 26 OCTOBER

DEPART :CALAIS          ( P&O EUROPEAN FERRIES REF p2041150)   AT 16:30

ARRIVE : DOVER EASTERN DOCK                                     AT 17:00

ARRIVE : SCHOOL                                                 AT 20:00

EMERGENCY CONTACT NO - 01273 320203 put you in touch with senior Equity staff outside office hours but should only be used in emergency.

St Mark's Square, Venice, Italy

Coach R204 WYD

**BERLIN STUDY VISIT – 5/11 NOVEMBER 2000**
ITINERARY by Coach

### SUNDAY, 5 NOVEMBER

| | |
|---|---|
| 14.00 | Meet at bus stop, Frenchay Campus |
| 14.30 | Depart from Frenchay Campus by coach (ISIS Educational Services emergency tel. no: 0370-810469; Priory Coaches tel: 01705 580522) |
| 18.45 | Arrive Dover |
| 18.45 | Check-in at Dover Eastern Docks (P&O ferry) |
| 19.45 | Depart on ferry |
| 21.30 | Arrive Calais, and travel overnight by coach (NB. Mainland Europe time is one hour forward of UK time) |

### MONDAY, 6 NOVEMBER

| | |
|---|---|
| 11.30 | Arrive Berlin, and check in at 13.00 to Hotel Econtel in Sömmeringstrasse 24-26, W-1000 Berlin (Tel: 00-49-30-346 810 & 346 81147; Fax: 00-49-30-346 81163; email: econtelcha@aol.com; internet: http://www.juwel-hotels.de ) |
| 15.00 | Optional guided tour of Berlin by Metro |
| 17.00 | Return to Hotel and rest of evening free |

### TUESDAY, 7 NOVEMBER

| | |
|---|---|
| 08.30 | Depart Hotel by coach to Potsdam |
| 09.30 | Tour by coach of Potsdam and Bornstedter Feld area |
| 10.30 | Visit by coach to Sanssouci Park |
| 12.00 | Visit by coach to Nauener Tor exhibition centre to view Potsdam development proposals |
| 13.00 | Return by coach to Fachhochschule Potsdam and lunch in the Mensa, Fachhochschule Potsdam |
| 14.00 | Room 1/1.02 - Presentation by Karsten Schröder of Entwicklungsträger Bornstedter Feld on proposals for regeneration of the Bornstedter Feld area of Potsdam |
| 15.00 | Site visit to the Kaserne Pappelallee northern sector with Karsten Schröder |
| 17.30 | Return by coach to Hotel |
| 18.30 | Rest of evening free in Berlin |

## WEDNESDAY, 8 NOVEMBER

| | |
|---|---|
| 08.30 | Depart Hotel by coach to Unter den Linden |
| 09.00 | Walk from Linden Corso in the Unter den Linden for guided tour by Richard Stott of SPD Savills of development projects down Friedrichstrasse to the American Business Centre |
| 10.00 | Walk from the American Business Centre & Checkpoint Charlie to Berlin Info Box |
| 10.30 | Arrive at Berlin Info Box for coffee and tour of the Berlin City Projects exhibition |
| 12.00 | Lunch at Berlin Info Box or Museum |
| 13.00 | Join coach at the Info Box and meet Neil Sutton (Chartered Quantity Surveyor of Gleeds GmbH) for guided tour of Deutsche Bahn project at Spreebogen |
| 14.00 | Return from Spreebogen, via Reichstag & Brandenburg Gate, to Berlin Info Box |
| 14.30 | Meet Mr Vasanth (Facilities Manager) at Berlin Info Box for guided tour of the Sony Project |
| 16.00 | Transfer by coach to Kurfürstenstrasse 84 for meeting at Berlin/ Brandenburg Property Owners and Developers Association (BFW) |
| 16.30 | Meet Wolfram Bielenstein, Marketing Manager with Balfour Beatty GmbH and BFW Managing Director, Frau Hiltrud Sprungala for presentation |
| 17.30 | Return by coach to Hotel |
| 18.00 | Arrive at Hotel and rest of evening free |

## THURSDAY, 9 NOVEMBER

| | |
|---|---|
| 08.30 | Depart Hotel by coach to Leipzig, south of Berlin |
| 11.00 | Site visit to the Petersbogen retail development in central Leipzig - led by Don Rosser of KIG Immobiliengesellscgaft mbH & Co (AMEC), including lunch and meeting with development and construction team members |
| 14.00 | Time to tour central Leipzig |
| 15.00 | Return by coach to Hotel |
| 17.30 | Arrive at Hotel |
| 18.30 | Meet at Hotel foyer to travel by Metro to restaurant |
| 19.00 | Meet at Restaurant at Rankstrasse 3 for Course Dinner – guest speaker David Lawrence Vice-President of Hanscomb GmbH |

## FRIDAY, 10 NOVEMBER

| | |
|---|---|
| | Morning & afternoon free in Berlin - check out of Hotel room by 11.00 and settle personal bills |
| 16.30 | Assemble in Hotel foyer |
| 17.00 | Depart Berlin, and travel overnight by coach |

## SATURDAY, 11 NOVEMBER

| | |
|---|---|
| 07.00 | Arrive Calais (stop at hypermarket) |
| 08.00 | Check in for P&O ferry |
| 09.30 | Depart Calais (Clocks go back one hour) |
| 09.45 | Arrive Folkestone |
| 14.00 | Arrive Frenchay Campus, UWE Bristol (and go home for a long sleep!) |

November 7th 2000
Coach R204WYD
Tour of Germany

*Below*: Berlin Wall

April 9th 2000, Claremont, South of France

Coach T764 JYB

April 10th 2000. New windscreen being fitted

April 14th 2000

Claremont Ferrand

Puy-de-Dome

April 14th 2000, Puy-de-Dome mountain

January 7th 2001, leaving Montgenevre

January 7th 2001, stopped to fit snow chains

Road from Claviere

February 2001. Road from Zerting to Schladming, Austria

A. Cooke sitting in his Igloo

Montgenevre Ski Resort

Coach T204 JYB

**TRAVEL AND ACCOMMODATION DETAILS**

SATURDAY 31 MARCH 2001

COACH OPERATED BY: PRIORY COACHES EMERGENCY TEL: 02392-580522
| DEPART | : SCHOOL | | AT 18:00 |
| ARRIVE | : FOLKESTONE EUROTUNNEL | | AT 21:00 |

| DEPART | : FOLKESTONE EUROTUNNEL | (EUROTUNNEL Ref: 64493299) | AT 21:51 |
| ARRIVE | : CALAIS EUROTUNNEL | | AT 23:26 |

SUNDAY 1 APRIL 2001

| DEPART | : CALAIS EUROTUNNEL |
| ARRIVE | : HOTEL – FRANCE |

| HOTEL | : Hotel Les Rois Mages |
| ADDRESS | : GRAND RUE |
| | : 05100 MONTGENEVRE |
| | : FRANCE |

TELEPHONE : 0033 492 219083

SATURDAY 7 APRIL 2001

| DEPART | : HOTEL – FRANCE | | AT 20:00 |
| ARRIVE | : CALAIS EUROTUNNEL | 8 APRIL | AT 08:30 |

| DEPART | : CALAIS EUROTUNNEL | (EUROTUNNEL Ref: 64493299) | AT 09:21 |
| ARRIVE | : FOLKESTONE EUROTUNNEL | | AT 08:56 |

| DEPART | : FOLKESTONE EUROTUNNEL | | AT 09:30 |
| ARRIVE | : SCHOOL | | AT 12:30 |

# PRIORY COACHES
## CYRIL COWDREY LTD.
**of** **GOSPORT**

Spirit of Silverstone

August 1st 2001

Coach R636 VYB

A day at the races

Coach T759 JYB

High Wycombe to Newcastle

October 1st for four nights

guided tours of Beamish village

Banbourge Castle, Crag House

and Catherine Cookson Country

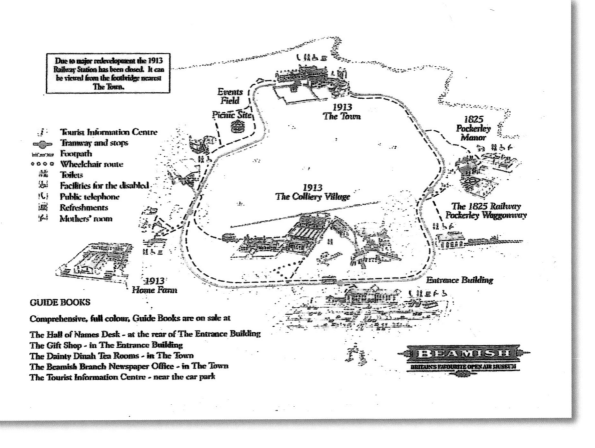

Due to major redevelopment the 1913 Railway Station has been closed. It can be viewed from the footbridge nearest The Town.

Events Field
Picnic Site
1913 The Town
1825 Pockerley Manor

*i*    Tourist Information Centre
Tramway and stops
Footpath
∘∘∘∘ Wheelchair route
Toilets
Facilities for the disabled
Public telephone
Refreshments
Mothers' room

1913 The Colliery Village

The 1825 Railway Pockerley Waggonway

1913 Home Farm

Entrance Building

**GUIDE BOOKS**

Comprehensive, full colour, Guide Books are on sale at

The Hall of Names Desk - at the rear of The Entrance Building
The Gift Shop - in The Entrance Building
The Dainty Dinah Tea Rooms - in The Town
The Beamish Branch Newspaper Office - in The Town
The Tourist Information Centre - near the car park

**BEAMISH**
BRITAIN'S FAVOURITE OPEN AIR MUSEUM

# LIST OF COACH REGISTRATIONS FOR THE FOLLOWING COMPANYS

## HIGHWAYS  TRAVEL COACHES

| | | | | |
|---|---|---|---|---|
| A700 CUF | ERP 18T | NEL 113P | UKH 874 | JHO 40P |
| A668 MJK | NJH 980R | RBW 177L | GMF 704J | |

------------------------------------------------------------

## PRIORY COACHES OF GOSPORT

| | | | | |
|---|---|---|---|---|
| M199 UYB | GFO 366 | D119 VFV | M212 UYD | L120 OWF |
| L680 MET | M216 UYD | M214 UYD | K807 EET | L860 MET |
| J214 UYD | MBZ 7136 | J461 JRV | M477 UYD | M199 UYD |
| P933 UYC | N709 CYC | 894 FUY | M477 UYA | R204 WYD |
| R636 UYB | E492 CPE | L982 OGY | L992 OGY | R636 VYB |
| P933 KYC | E986 NMK | R204 WRO | S749 XYA | RJI 8726 |
| T758 JYB | T759 JYB | T763 JYB | T764 JYB | M636 UYB |
| FSU 803 | P424PBP | M199 VYB | P938 KYC | |
| Double Deckers | | PSU 951 | C381 NHJ | RJI 8610 |

------------------------------------------------------------

## HELLYERS COACHES OF FAREHAM

| | | | | |
|---|---|---|---|---|
| R636 VYB | T763 JYB | X4 HOF | A16 HOF | A13 HOF |
| SA02 UGN | M665 KVU | M214 UYD | HF03 HOF | R204 WYD |
| A8 HOF | A19 HOF | W2 HOF | P933 KYC | Y 14 HOF |
| A17 HOF | S749 XYA | TJI 4926 | P49JJU | A12 HOF |
| A18 HOF | A16 HOF | N214 UYD | M477 UYA | X10 HOF |
| P953 DNR | UF 03 HOF | M204 UYD | B10 HOF | LVS 441V |
| Y10 HOF | JF 04 HOF | YN51 MFZ | R146 COR | A3 HFU |
| A20 HOF | A6 HFN | A14 HFY | M664 KVU | A4 HFY |
| SF05 HOF | T759 JYB | | | |

------------------------------------------------------------

# COACH REGISTRATIONS CONTINUED

## ZENITH TRAVEL OF LEE ON SOLENT

| | | | | |
|---|---|---|---|---|
| YIL2185 | CEZ 5242 | CEZ 5292 | CLZ 1830 | S921 TVZ |
| F76 SMC | CEZ5290 | M902 WNO | CEZ 5252 | HIL 6575 |

-------------------------------------------------------------------

## LUCKETTS TRAVEL OF FAREHAM

A13 HLC        A16 HOF        YR02 ZZB        807 SDT        N626 PUS
A4 SDL        W5 HLC        YS03 ZLK        R4 HLC        V200
RAD  A19 LTG        Y2 HLC        KBZ 2276        R871 SDT
HX03 BYT  W3 HLC        W2 HLC        P844 WUG        Y4 HLC
YR52 MDV  P953 DNR        R887 SDT

-------------------------------------------------------------------

## VISION TRAVEL OF BEDHAMPTON

YS03 ZLE        W136 OSM        VZ 9177        SA02 UGN        9508 VT
VIL 9765        VIL8671        YN04 GFV        TIL 2720        W16
OSM  VIL 9346        VIL 6286        P70 SEL        P628 ADG
VIL 9516  VZ 1673        VIL 2915        S576 ACT        GIL 8674
P600 MPY BZ 1673        VX06 AEM        Y698 KSF        P500 MPY
P400 MPY  VIL 1590        P300 MPY        P700 MPY        P198 TWX
VIL 9237  YN05 BUP        VIL 2226        EX53 UOC        VIL 5305

-------------------------------------------------------------------

# EXCELSIOR

## TOURS AND EXCURSIONS

**THE MILLENNIUM DOME
At Greenwich**

'The Experience of a Lifetime'

### London Excursions

# EXCELSIOR OF PORTSMOUTH

Continental Tours

Started with T.G. M on 11th October 2001

First journey Southsea to London, Coach A6 EXC

# TELLINGS · GOLDEN MILLER
## COACHES LIMITED

*No.1 in Coach Travel*

| | | | |
|---|---|---|---|
| **LB52 UYK** | | | |
| **KU02 YUF** | **DUTY** | **SERVICE** | **ROUTE** |
| **KU02 YUG** | 1 | 030 | LONDON VIA GUILDFORD |
| **KP51 SYF** | 2 | 030 | LONDON VIA ALTON |
| **KP51 UEV** | 3 | 030 | LONDON VIA FAREHAM, HEATHROW |
| **KP51 UEW** | 4 | 032 | LONDON |
| **KP51 UEX** | 5 | 032 | LONDON VIA SOUTHAMPTON |
| **KP51 UEY** | 6 | 030 | PORTSMOUTH |
| **KP51 UEZ** | 7 | 030 | PORTSMOUTH |
| **R10 TGM** | 8 | 030 | PORTSMOUTH |
| **R20 TGM** | 9 | 030 | SOUTHSEA VIA GUILDFORD |
| **R584 GDX** | 10 | 032 | PORTSMOUTH |
| **R595 GDX** | 11 | 032 | PORTSMOUTH VIA SOUTHAMPTON |
| **R177 TKU** | 12 | 032 | SOUTHAMPTON |
| **R188 TKU** | 13 | 300 | BRISTOL |
| | 14 | 300 | BRISTOL VIA ALL STOPS |
| | 15 | 300 | SOUTHSEA |

TELLINGS GOLDEN MILLER
PORTSMOUTH
DUTY SHEET
**DUTY 21**

*DAILY*

*SUMMER TIMETABLE*

**SERVICE 310**

**DRIVER BOOK ON 0845HRS (CHECK OIL & WATER)**

Take coach to TLC Travel Ltd, Linton Street, Bradford. Drop toilet/recharge tank and clean coach ready for return journey, depart yard at 0945hrs for Bradford Interchange.

0955   BRADFORD **INTERCHANGE DEP**
1025   LEEDS **BUS & COACH STATION (DYER STREET) ARR**
1030   LEEDS **BUS & COACH STATION (DYER STREET) DEP**
1110   SHEFFIELD **(MEADOWHALL) INTERCHANGE**
1125   SHEFFIELD **INTERCHANGE ARR**
1130   SHEFFIELD **INTERCHANGE DEP**
1200   CHESTERFIELD **BUS STATION (BEETWELL STREET)**
1245   NOTTINGHAM **BROAD MARSH BUS STATION ARR**
1250   NOTTINGHAM **BROAD MARSH BUS STATION DEP**
1335   LEICESTER **ST MARGARET'S BUS STATION ARR**

      <u>(TAKE A 40 MIN BREAK AS PER TIMETABLE)</u>

1415   LEICESTER **ST MARGARET'S BUS STATION DEP**
1500   COVENTRY **POOL MEADOW BUS STATION ARR**
1505   COVENTRY **POOL MEADOW BUS STATION DEP**
1525   LEAMINGTON SPA **(HOLLY WALK, HAMILTON TERRACE)**
1600   BANBURY **BUS STATION (BRIDGE STREET)**
1650   OXFORD **BUS STATION (GLOUCESTER GREEN) ARR**

      <u>(TAKE A 40 MIN BREAK AS PER TIMETABLE)</u>

1730   OXFORD **BUS STATION (GLOUCESTER GREEN) DEP**
1825   READING-CALCOT **(SAVACENTRE M4 JUNCTION 12)**
1855   BASINGSTOKE **BUS STATION**
1945   FAREHAM **BUS STATION**
2000   PORTSMOUTH **CONTINENTAL FERRYPORT**
2005   PORTSMOUTH **THE HARD INTERCHANGE**
2010   SOUTHSEA **CLARENCE PIER**
2015   SOUTHSEA **SOUTH PARADE PIER**

TELLINGS GOLDEN MILLER
PORTSMOUTH
DUTY SHEET

**DUTY 20A**                                          **SERVICE 310**

**DRIVER BOOK ON 0730HRS (CHECK OIL & WATER)**

0800  SOUTHSEA **SOUTH PARADE PIER**
0805  SOUTHSEA **CLARENCE PIER**
0815  PORTSMOUTH **THE HARD INTERCHANGE**
0820  PORTSMOUTH **CONTINENTAL FERRYPORT**
0835  FAREHAM **BUS STATION**
0930  BASINGSTOKE **BUS STATION**
1000  READING – CALCOT **(SAVACENTRE M4 JUNC. 12)**
1050  OXFORD BUS STATION **(GLOUCESTER GREEN) ARR**

(TAKE A40 MIN BREAK AS PER TIMETABLE)

1130  OXFORD **(GLOUCESTER GREEN) DEP**
1210  BANBURY **BUS STATION (BRIDGE STREET)**
1240  LEAMINGTON SPA **(HOLLY WALK, HAMILTON TERRACE)**
1305  COVENTRY **POOL MEADOW BUS STATION ARR**
1310  COVENTRY **POOL MEADOW BUS STATION DEP**
1400  LEICESTER **ST MARGARET'S BUS STATION ARR**

(TAKE A 40 MIN BREAK AS PER TIMETABLE)

1440  LEICESTER **ST MARGARET'S BUS STATION DEP**
1525  NOTTINGHAM **BROAD MARSH BUS STATION ARR**
1530  NOTTINGHAM **BROAD MARSH BUS STATION DEP**
1610  CHESTERFIELD **BUS STATION (BEETWELL STREET)**
1640  SHEFFIELD **INTERCHANGE ARR**
1645  SHEFFIELD **INTERCHANGE DEP**
1700  SHEFFIELD **(MEADOW HALL) INTERCHANGE**
1740  LEEDS **COACH & BUS STATION (DYER STREET) ARR**
1745  LEEDS **COACH & BUS STATION (DYER STREET) DEP**
1815  BRADFORD **INTERCHANGE**

## Tellings-Golden Miller SG

The latest Caetano Nimbus-bodied Dennis Darts have started to arrive. They are B32D-bodied 428-33 (RL02 FOT/U, FVM/N, ZTB/C). As expected, Dennis Darts P290-6 FPK have returned to Arriva Southern Counties.

## Thames Travel, Wallingford

The Leyland Lynx referred to in August Fleet News was on loan only to cover for temporarily disabled former Ipswich Dennis/East Lancs YDX 104Y. Scania L94UB/Wright Solar YP02 ABN was on loan but was considered too long for this fleet.

Recent deliveries to Tellings-Golden Miller include KU02 YUF, a Volvo B12M/Plaxton Paragon for the Portsmouth-Leeds National Express service. It was photographed in Chesterfield.

Driver : A. COOKE

# T.G.M

## NATIONAL EXPRESS SERVICES

## LONDON VICTORIA RETURN

**SUMMER 2004**

***TELLINGS GOLDEN MILLER***
***PORTSMOUTH***

**DUTY 2**

**MON - FRI**
**SERVICE 030**

**DRIVER REPORTS 0515**

| | |
|---|---|
| 0545 | PORTSMOUTH (THE HARD INTERCHANGE) |
| 0550 | PORTSMOUTH (CONTINENTAL FERRYPORT) |
| 0555 | HILSEA |
| 0557 | COSHAM |
| 0559 | WIDLEY |
| 0602 | PURBROOK |
| 0605 | WATERLOOVILLE |
| 0607 | COWPLAIN |
| 0610 | HORNDEAN |
| 0630 | HINDHEAD |
| 0650 | GUILDFORD (Park Barn) |
| 0800 | LONDON (WANDSWORTH, ARMOURY WAY. STOP D) |
| 0820 | LONDON (VICTORIA) |

**Please Note**
**Park in departures ,but not before 0830.**

**RETURN JOURNEY**                                **SERVICE 032**

| | | |
|---|---|---|
| 0900 | LONDON (VICTORIA) | |
| 0945 | HEATHROW (Central Bus Station) | |
| 1035 | BASINGSTOKE BUS STATION | **STAND 1** |
| 1105 | WINCHESTER | |
| 1140 | SOUTHAMPTON COACH STATION | |
| 1145 | RED FUNNEL FERRY TERMINAL | |
| 1210 | FAREHAM | |
| 1225 | PORTSMOUTH (CONTINENTAL FERRYPORT) | |
| 1230 | PORTSMOUTH (THE HARD INTERCHANGE) | |

# T.G.M

# NATIOAL EXPRESS SERVICE

# 316 - PERRANPORTH

SUMMER 2005

*TELLINGS GOLDEN MILLER*
*PORTSMOUTH*
<u>DUTY 22</u>                                              <u>DAILY</u>
                                                     <u>*SERVICE 316*</u>

DRIVER BOOK ON 0800 HRS

0825    PORTSMOUTH THE HARD INTERCHANGE
0830    PORTSMOUTH Continental Ferryport
0845    FAREHAM BUS STATION
0920    SOUTHAMPTON COACH STATION
0950    RINGWOOD Meeting House Lane STAND A
1010    ARR. BOURNEMOUTH TRAVEL INTERCHANGE
(TAKE A 50 MINUTE BREAK AS PER TIMETABLE

1100    DEP. BOURNEMOUTH TRAVEL INTERCHANGE
1108    BRANKSOME Poole Rd.Opp.Courts Superstore
1120    POOLE Dolphin Cntr. Bus Station
1135    WAREHAM North St. Post Office
1215    WEYMOUTH Kings Statne Stand K7
1235    DORCHESTER South Rail Station
1305    ARR. BRIDPORT COACH PARK West St.
(TAKE A 20 MINUTE BREAK AS PER TIMETABLE)

1325    DEP. BRIDPORT COACH PARK West St.
1430    ARR. EXETER BUS & COACH STATION Paris St.
1435    DEP. EXETER BUS & COACH STATION Paris St.
1540    ARR. PLYMOUTH BUS STATION Bretonside
(TAKE A 50 MINUTE BREAK AS PER TIMETABLE)

1630    DEP. PLYMOUTH BUS STATION Bretonside
1637    PLYMOUTH Milehouse Bus Depot
1642    PLYMOUTH St Budeaux Sq. Opp. Warrens Bakery
1645    SALTASH North Rd
1648    BURRATON Shell Garage
1652    LANDRAKE By-Pass Bus Stop
1655    TIDEFORD Bus Shelter Main Rd
1705    LISKEARD Barras St. Post Office
1710    DOBWALLS Opp. Post Office
1730    BODMIN Priory Rd. Opp. St Petroc's Church
1745    WADEBRIDGE Link Rd. Opp. Lidl
1800    ST COLUMB MAJOR Cattle Mkt.
1810    ST COLUMB MINOR Turn Junc. Church St.
1811    NEWQUAY Porthfour Turn
1815    ARR.NEWQUAY BUS STATION Coach Bay
1820    DEP. NEWQUAY BUS STATION Coach Bay
1835    GOONHAVEN Opp. Bus Shelter
1840    PERRAN SANDS Haven Holiday Centre
1845    PERRANPORTH Beach Rd.

# Tellings-Golden- Miller of Portsmouth

## NATIONAL EXPRESS - WAYFARER STAGE NUMBERS
### Commencing 25 March 2002

| ROUTE: 030 | | ROUTE: 032 | | ROUTE: 035 | |
| --- | --- | --- | --- | --- | --- |
| STAGE NO. | STOP | STAGE NO. | STOP | STAGE NO. | STOP |
| 1 | LONDON VICTORIA | 1 | LONDON VICTORIA | 1 | LONDON VICTORIA |
| 2 | Putney | 3 | HEATHROW AIRPORT | 2 | Hammersmith |
| 3 | HEATHROW AIRPORT | 4 | BASINGSTOKE | 3 | HEATHROW AIRPORT |
| 4 | Farnborough | 5 | Brighton Hill | 7 | Winchester |
| 5 | ALDERSHOT | 6 | Kempshott | 9 | Bassett Crossroads |
| 6 | Farnham | 7 | WINCHESTER | 10 | SOUTHAMPTON |
| 7 | Alton | 9 | Bassett Crossroads | 49 | Ringwood |
| 8 | West Meon | 10 | SOUTHAMPTON | 50 | BOURNEMOUTH |
| 9 | Droxford | 11 | Red Funnel Terminal | 51 | Westbourne |
| 10 | Wickham | 24 | FAREHAM | 52 | Branksome |
| 11 | GUILDFORD | 29 | Portsmouth CFT | 53 | Parkstone |
| 12 | Hindhead | 30 | PORTSMOUTH | 55 | POOLE |
| 13 | Liphook | 33 | West Wellow | 56 | Wareham |
| 14 | Rake | 34 | SALISBURY | 57 | Corfe Castle |
| 15 | PETERSFIELD | 35 | Lyndhurst | 58 | SWANAGE |
| 16 | Horndean | 36 | Brockenhurst | 59 | Dorchester |
| 17 | Cowplain | 37 | LYMINGTON | 60 | WEYMOUTH |
| 18 | Waterlooville | 38 | Everton Corner | | |

| ROUTE: 033 | |
| --- | --- |
| STAGE NO. | STOP |
| 1 | LONDON VICTORIA |
| 3 | HEATHROW AIRPORT |
| 5 | Andover |
| 6 | Amesbury |
| 34 | SALISBURY |
| 35 | Wilton |
| 36 | Shaftesbury |
| 37 | Gillingham |
| 38 | Henstridge |
| 39 | Milborne Port |
| 40 | Sherborne |
| 41 | YEOVIL |

| 19 | Purbrook | 39 | Milford on Sea |
| --- | --- | --- | --- |
| 20 | Widley | 40 | New Milton |
| 21 | Cosham | 41 | Highcliffe |
| 22 | Havant | 42 | Christchurch |
| 23 | Hilsea | 43 | Boscombe |
| 24 | FAREHAM | 49 | Ringwood |
| 29 | Portsmouth CFT | 50 | BOURNEMOUTH |
| 30 | PORTSMOUTH | 51 | Westbourne |
| 31 | Southsea Clarence Pier | 52 | Branksome |
| 32 | SOUTHSEA S PARADE | 53 | Parkstone |
| | | 55 | POOLE |

---

**BOURNEMOUTH TRANSPORT DRIVERS PLEASE NOTE:**
YOU MUST USE SERVICE NUMBERS 130, 132 or 135 ON WAYFARER TICKET MACHINE

# TGM depots

Issue date: June 2002

## The Old Tram Garage, Twickenham, Middlesex

| Bus Fleet  93 | Peak Vehicle Requirement 83 |
|---|---|
| Ferry Vehicles  16 | |

Fleet make up 7 Volvo B10BLE Alexander, 1 Mercedes 709 Plaxton Beaver
8 Optare Excels, 77 Dennis Darts all Plaxton Pointer with the exception of
7 Caetano Nimbus.

| Staff Numbers | 204 full time drivers |
|---|---|
| | 15 part time drivers |
| | 30 casual drivers |

Routes operated 203,235,465,490,726,H20, H21, H25, H26, H28, R62, R68, and R70.

| Coach Fleet   32 |
|---|

Fleet Make up  7 Setra 315GTHD, 2 Iveco Beulas, 3 Volvo Van Hool
2 Volvo Caetano, 1 Toyota Caetano, 17 Volvo Plaxtons

| Staff numbers | 40 Full time drivers |
|---|---|
| | 12 part time drivers |

Operations Private Hire, Tours Excursions, European Tours and
School Contract Services.

## Wintersells Road Byfleet

| Bus Fleet  41 | Peak Vehicle Requirement 38 |
|---|---|
| Ferry 2 | |

Fleet Make up 11 Dennis Darts Plaxton Pointer with the exception of
2 Caetano Compasses, 32 Mercedes Plaxton Beavers

| Staff Numbers | 62 Full Time Drivers |
|---|---|
| | 5 Part time drivers |

Type of operations Mainly tendered bus routes for Surrey County Council and
Kingston University together with a Commercial Route and numerous
School Contract services.

Routes Operated 48,81,218,400,437,438,441,442,446,471,472,478,513,514,515,
564,566,567,637,662, 663,667,678,803,KU1 and KU2.

## Fratton Road, Portsmouth

| Coach Fleet  11 |
|---|

Fleet Make up 3 x Volvo/Van Hool's, 1 Volvo/Plaxton Premiere,  2 x Volvo/
Plaxton Paragon's & 5 Volvo/Plaxton Panthers

| Staff Numbers | 22 Full Time Drivers |
|---|---|
| | 2 Part time Drivers |

Type of operations Contracted services for National Express from Portsmouth
to London, Bristol and Bradford.

Routes operated 030,032,300 and 310

Arrived Bristol

Parked up

## National Express — 10 trip Multiride

| Date  |  |  |  |  |  |  |  |  |  |  |
|-------|--|--|--|--|--|--|--|--|--|--|
| Time  |  |  |  |  |  |  |  |  |  |  |
| Route |  |  |  |  |  |  |  |  |  |  |
| Ref.  |  |  |  |  |  |  |  |  |  |  |

This ticket is valid for 10 single journeys in either direction, during the advertised period of validity.
Unreserved tickets do not guarantee travel on any specific journey.
Reservations are available for an additional charge. Issued subject to National Express conditions.

Information: 08705 80 80 80 | www.nationalexpress.com | Emergencies: 0121 625 1278 (24 hours)
National Express Customer Services, PO Box 9854, Birmingham B16 8XN

# AUSTRALIA

# MY HOLIDAY DREAM

## October 4th 2002

## The start of my Australian holiday

## (My dream of a lifetime)

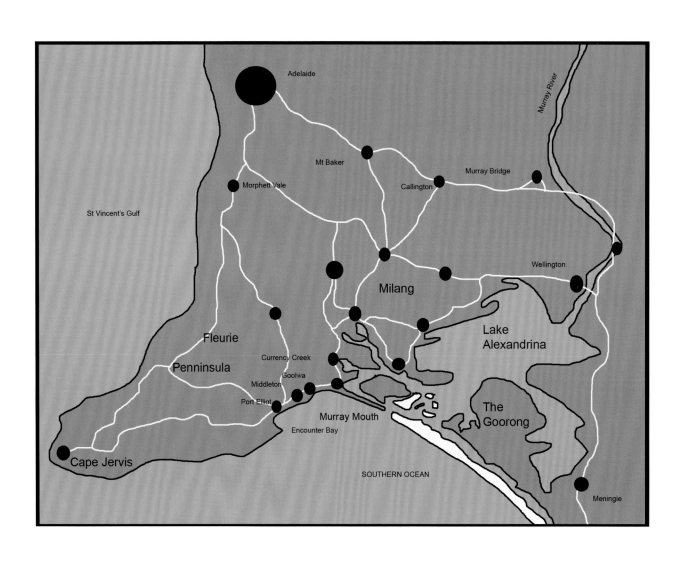

## Australia October 7th 2002

During a tour around Adelaide, I discovered a red
London double decker bus, registration number SGH 736,
advertising London bus tours on the front and sides.

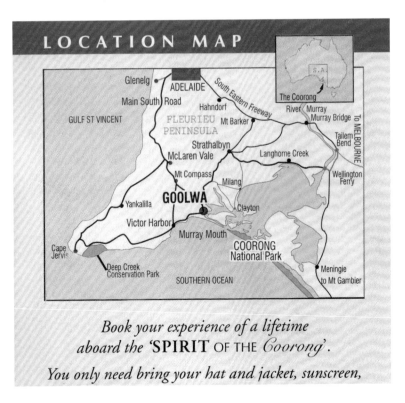

# My Australian holiday

Based at Goolwa, near Adelaide, close to Victor Harbour

Visited Sovereign Hill Gold Mine 15th October overnight stay at the Arch Motel Ballarat

# Nat Express makes tracks out of Victoria

**By David Heller**
**Chief City Correspondent**

NATIONAL EXPRESS, the trains, buses and coaches group, yesterday announced a costly retreat from its train and tram operations in Australia.

The move by National Express will involve a £135 million depreciation, comprising a potential £48 million cash payment to indemnify the providers of performance bonds and an £87 million non-cash asset write-down.

The group said the withdrawal from train and tram operations in the state of Victoria would not affect its bus operations in Melbourne, Brisbane, Sydney and Perth. However, some analysts predicted the group might eventually withdraw from Australia entirely.

The train and tram operations recorded an operating loss of £2.3 million in the first half of the year in spite of receiving a £16.5 million state subsidy.

"After a year of negotiation, we have concluded we are not prepared to fund losses on these operations as we are unable — despite significant efforts by the Victoria government and ourselves — to reach a revised financial arrangement with the government without incurring an unacceptable level of operational and financial risk from next year onwards," a statement from the company said.

National Express said there was no link between its partial withdrawal from its Australian business and the departure earlier this month of finance direc-

DEPARTURE: National Express will no longer provide tram services in the state of Victoria

tor William Rollason. Chief executive Phil White said the group was in talks with the Australian government with a view to providing an orderly handover of its train and tram operations to keep disruption to a minimum for both passengers and employees. Earlier this

year, National Express complained about the high level of fare evasion on some of its Australian services.

In the UK, said the company, rail passenger growth remained static during the year, while both bus operations and the UK coach divi-

sion reported good progress. The group said its new school year in North America and Canada had started well.

It is focusing on reducing costs in the public transit division.

National Express shares closed down 14½p at 405p.

National Express announce its withdrawal of tram and train operations in 'Victoria', Australia

# Hellyers Vehicle List

**Hellyers**
of Fareham

Here is our complete Vehicle list as at May 2004

| Chassis | Bodywork | Specification | Seats | Numb |
|---------|----------|---------------|-------|------|
| **Setra (Mercedes Benz)** | S415 HD | Luxury Air Conditioned Executive | 49 | |
| | S315GT-HD | Air Conditioned Executive | 49 | |
| **Mercedes Benz** | Hispani Vita | Air Conditioned Executive | 49 | |
| **Scania** | Irizar Century | Air Conditioned Executive | 49 | |
| | Van Hool Alizee | Air Conditioned Executive | 49 | |
| | Van Hool Alizee | Executive | 49 | |
| | Plaxton Premiere 320 | Standard | 53 | |
| **Volvo** | Jonkheere Mistral | Air Conditioned Executive | 49 | |
| | Jonkheere Mistral | Air Conditioned Executive | 51 | |
| | Jonkheere Deauville | Standard | 53 | |
| | Plaxton Premier 350 | Standard | 53 | |
| | Plaxton Excalibur | Executive | 49 | |
| | Plaxton Paramount 3500 | Standard | 57 | |
| | Van Hool Alizee | Executive | 46 | |
| **DAF** | Bova Futura FHD | Air Conditioned Executive | 49 | |
| | | Air Conditioned Executive | 36 | |
| | | Air Conditioned | 45 | |
| | | Standard | 53 | |
| | Bova Futura FLD | Standard | 57 | |
| | | Standard | 53 | |
| **Dennis** | Plaxton 3200 | Standard | 57 | |
| | Plaxton Pointer | Low Floored Bus | 39 seated 22 standing | |
| **Toyota** | Salvador Caetano | Standard | 21 | |
| **Mercedes** | Mercedes 814D | Standard | 24 | |
| | Vito | Standard | 7 | |
| **Leyland** | Van Hool Alizee | Executive | 50 | |
| | Plaxton Supreme | Standard | 51 | |
| | | Standard | 53 | |

July 4th 2004 Coach M665 KVU

The Wirral Birkenhead to Betws-y-Coed

July 13th 2004 Konigsee, Austria. Depart from here by boat to St
Bartholoma then on to Salt Mines at Berchtesgaden

# HELLYERS

# 4 Day tour to Saint Omer

## COACH OPERATOR

HELLYERS OF FAREHAM LTD
FORT FAREHAM BUSINESS PARK
NEWGATE LANE
FAREHAM
HANTS PO14 1AH
TEL : 01329 285432/7
FAX : 01329 235267
EMERGENCY TEL : 07836 690678 01329 285437
**COACH TYPE : STANDARD COACH WITH 1 DRIVER**

## OPERATOR OUT

EUROTUNNEL
COACH SALES CENTRE
EUROTUNNEL
PO BOX 300
FOLKESTONE
KENT
CT19 4QD
TEL :- 0870 2430401
FAX :- 01303 288909
BOOKING REFERENCE :- 09460676

## OPERATOR IN

EUROTUNNEL
COACH SALES CENTRE
EUROTUNNEL
PO BOX 300
FOLKESTONE
KENT
CT19 4QD
TEL :- 0870 2430401
FAX :- 01303 288909
BOOKING REFERENCE :- 09460676

## ACCOMMODATION DETAILS

LA GAREYNE EBBLINGHEM
LIEUDIT KASTEL VELT
RN 42
59173 EBBLINGHEM
SAINT OMER
FRANCE
TEL: 00 33 3 28 44 22 10
FAX: 00 33 3 28 44 22 11
**TEACHERS ROOM TELEPHONE: 00 33 3 28 44 22 16 – INCOMING CALLS ONLY**

**PLEASE REMEMBER TO TAKE TOWELS AND TOILETRIES FROM HOME AS THESE ARE NOT PROVIDED EXCEPT FOR ONE LARGE TOWEL PER ADULT**

**PLEASE LIAISE CLOSELY WITH YOUR DRIVER REGARDING ANY TRANSFERS OR PICKUPS THAT YOU MAY REQUIRE DURING THE TOUR. PLEASE ALSO NOTE THAT YOUR TOUR MUST COMPLY WITH DRIVERS' HOURS REGULATIONS AND THAT YOUR DRIVER'S DECISION IS FINAL.**

## Sunday 18 July 2004

The group will be met at school by their coach at 12:30 hrs to load luggage ready for departure by 13:00 hrs en route for Folkestone. We would suggest that the group take provisions from home for the journey and suitable stops will be made en route as necessary.

It is requested that the group report to the Eurotunnel Terminal, Folkestone by 13:30 hrs for the 14:36 hrs crossing to Calais.

This crossing will take 35 minutes, however as watches should be advanced one hour during the crossing for continental time, arrival into Calais is expected at 16:11 hrs.

The group will disembark and continue the journey to **Ebblinghem** where accommodation has been arranged at La Gareyne Ebblinghem.

**Ebblinghem** is a small rural village only a 15 minute drive from St Omer. Ebblinghem had associations with military training camps during WW1 and WW2 and on the outskirts of the village there is a British Military Cemetery.

Arrival is anticipated at approximately 17:15 hrs. Here the group will spend the next 3 nights with Full Board accommodation commencing with dinner this evening. The group will require organised activities after the meal.

*If arrival time is going to be earlier or later than shown above please telephone the manager at Le Chateau.*

## Monday 19 July 2004

The group will board their coach following breakfast and travel to **St Omer** where they plan to carry out the **NST Town Treasure Trail.** Packed lunches provided.

*PLEASE NOTE: Most of the shops in St Omer are closed on Mondays.*

**St. Omer:** a quiet and attractive town set on hills between the canals. From 12 October 1914 to the 30 April 1916 the British General Headquarters was based here. In 1917 it became the Royal Flying Corps and Royal Air Force Headquarters until the end of the war.
Now St Omer has the special charm of an old town with a series of small streets, most of which are pedestrian or semi-pedestrian.
Of interest in the town is the magnificent Notre-Dame Cathedral dating back to the 12th and 14th centuries and the Municipal Fine Arts Museum. Just a few yards from the town centre is one of the finest public parks in the region with more than 20 hectares to ramble through. It also contains a large outdoor swimming pool which is open in July and August only.

The group will continue to **La Coupole** where a visit has been **confirmed** for the group at **11:15 hours.**

La Coupole, St Omer. 2004 Group Prices: **Adults: 7,00 euros. Children up to 16: 4,00 euros.** Telephone: 00 33 3 21 93 07 07. Fax: 00 33 3 21 39 21 45. *Web site address*: http://www.lacoupole.com **Please note credit cards are accepted.**

Here in a most impressive underground V2 base you will discover the hidden facets of World War II and the conquest of Space. Go back in time to witness the living conditions under the German occupation of France and re-live the main events of the post-war conquest of Space from the first Sputnik to the Apollo missions. The Centre displays the latest museographic technology and guided visits using headsets are available. After your visit lifts will take you down to the lower galleries. Here you will find yourself at the heart of an unfinished building site at the foot of impressive 15m high concrete walls. This is the polygon, the launching pad complex for the V2s. *Please take some warm clothing as it can be cold in the lower galleries.*

**Ensure that each pupil has a pencil. Clipboards are available at reception on request to help the pupils take notes. La Coupole prefer pupils not to take bags into this visit.**

*There is a drivers rest room at La Coupole.*

The group will proceed by coach to **Eperlecques.**

**Bunker d'Eperlecques, 62910 Eperlecques (A26 Exit Nordausques on D221). Here a visit has been requested for the group at 14:45 hours.** Telephone: 03 21 88 44 22. Fax: 03 21 88 44 84. This bunker which survived the 1943 bombings forms the backdrop to a history lesson about the Second World War. Wall displays present the world at war while a commentary explains why this strategic place was chosen. The technology of the V1 and V2 rockets and the construction techniques used to build the bunker are explained.
**2004 Group Prices: 3.70 Euros per pupil. Adults free of charge.** *Credit cards not accepted.*

The group will return to Le Chateau for evening meal followed by activities organised by Le Chateau staff.


## Tuesday 20 July 2004

The group will have an **early breakfast** and depart on their coach for a full days visit to **Disneyland Paris.** Packed lunches provided. *Please note that packed lunches cannot be taken into Disneyland. A picnic area is situated outside the Park.*

**Your driver will advise the time of departure today but it is anticipated as being approximately 08:00 hours.**

**The Disneyland Paris Resort** covers some 1943 hectares, (an area equal to one-fifth the surface of Paris), complete with the Disneyland Paris Theme Park, six hotels, an 18 hole golf course, camping sites, tennis courts, shops, restaurants and a night time entertainment centre covering 18,000 square metres. The resort will be open 365 days a year. There are 5 Theme Parks within the resort, Main Street USA, Frontierland, Adventureland, Fantasyland and Discoveryland.

**Pre-paid tickets have been requested for this visit.**

There are coach driver facilities now installed in the coach park area, there are group windows designed to service group requirements. For the drivers there are facilities in the parking area which include a meeting point, TV room, reading room, games room and also a rest room. There are also shower and toilet facilities. A restaurant has also been built in this area.

**Your driver will advise the departure time from Disneyland.**

The group will return to Le Chateau for a **late** evening meal. Due to the late return organised activities may not be available.


# Wednesday 21 July 2004

The group will vacate their rooms after breakfast and load luggage onto the coach ready for departure on the homeward journey. Packed lunches will be provided on departure (last meal included in the tour cost).

The group will travel to **Boulogne** this morning.

*Boulogne: Boulogne was flourishing in Roman times when Julius Caesar used the area as a base for his invasion of Britain. Centuries later the town was occupied by the English, but returned to the French Crown in 1550. Today Boulogne is rich in monuments and reminders of the glorious past. Of special interest in the Old Town are the Ramparts which date back to the 13th century, the Town Hall with its 13th century Belfry and the Cathedral, which was built in 1827. Also of interest is the Imperial Palace; the Palais de Justice, the Fine Art Archaeology Museum situated in Grande Rue and the Colonne de la Grande Armee - surmounted by a statue of Napoleon, Boulogne's highest monument.*

**Markets are held in Boulogne on Wednesday mornings in Place Dalton.** *Fireworks, laser pens, penknives, small pets etc are all available for sale at French markets. Could you please advise your pupils that these items would be confiscated at customs if purchased.*

*Coach parking is available near Nausicaa. Please note that this is approximately 15 minutes walk away from the Town Square and market areas. We are advised that there is also parking available near the old town area.*

**A visit to the Nausicaa Marine Centre,** Boulevard Sainte-Beuve, 62200 Boulogne-sur-Mer (Tel: 03 21 30 99 99) **has been confirmed for 10:15 hrs. 2004 Group prices: Pupil 7 Euros; 1:10 free; Extra Adults 10 Euros.** *Payment by credit card accepted.*

Nausicaa Sea Life Centre has 15,000 square metres of exhibitions and activities, 1,400 cubic metres of aquariums with over 4,000 fish. See the wonderful world of the sea in films and documentaries. Walk through the shark corridor and venture deeper into the world of the tuna. Stroke fish who have no fear of man and test your knowledge of the world of the sea. From anemone fish to scavenging shrimps, plankton and the many inhabitants of sunken wrecks the sea world of Nausicaa awaits your discovery.

To back up project work, **Nausicaa's Education Service** is staffed by teachers and organisers and offers a variety of teaching aids for sale to help you plan a visit of educational value. For information telephone: 0033 3 21 30 99 83 or email: education@nausicaa.fr

The group will spend some leisure time in **Boulogne.** A copy of the **NST Town Treasure Trail** has been provided.

It is requested that the group report to the Eurotunnel Terminal, Calais by 15:30 hrs for the 16:31 hrs crossing to Folkestone.

This crossing will take 35 minutes and as watches should be put back one hour during the crossing for BST/GMT arrival into Folkestone is anticipated at 16:06 hrs. After Customs formalities, the group will continue their homeward journey with arrival back at school expected at approximately 16:30 hrs .

July 30th 2004

Coach R204 WYD

Goodwood Races

August 9th 2006. View from Coach Y10 H0F on the Jurassic coast road to Perranporth. Dinosaur & Egg sculpture.

August 2004. Border view of Southshields on way to Edinburgh Tattoo and visit to York Minster on return.

# York Minster

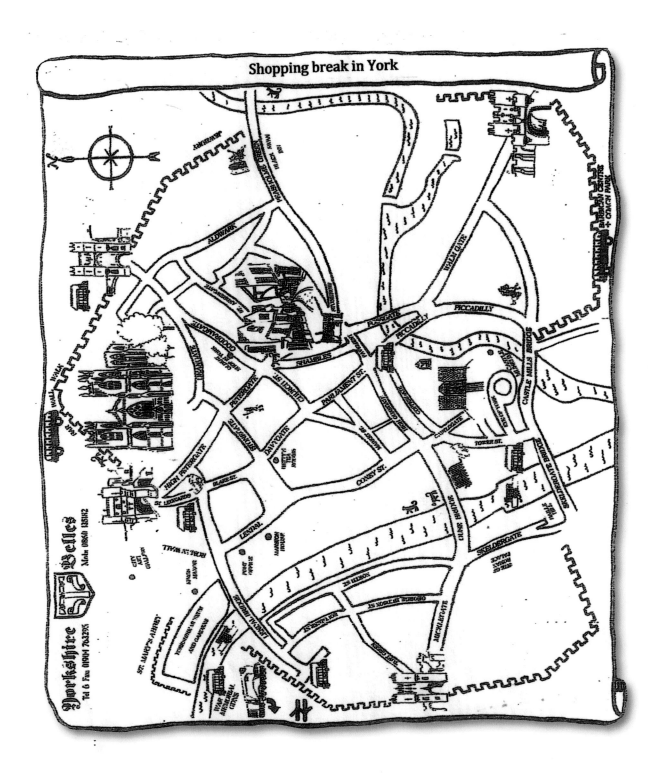

| Company Background | Private Hire | UK & Continental Touring | Excursions & Holiday Programme | Contract Hire | Vehicle List | Maintenance Facilities |
|---|---|---|---|---|---|---|

**O**ur vehicles are available for hire on every day of the year. We receive requests for a wide variety of activities including school outings, theatre trips, social club functions, airport transfers, sporting events and business trips. We are able to complement these services by providing booking facilities for cross-channel ferry or shuttle services or venues such as theme parks, exhibitions, theatres and restaurants.

We have developed our excellent reputation by remaining committed to providing our customers with a reliable service of the highest quality.

We will continue to do this and we will strive to improve our reputation and service even further

*Coach Hire for all occasions*

August 15th 2004

Alnwick Castle, Northumberland

August 13th 2004
Peebles.

August 14th Barony Castle
on way to Edinburgh Tattoo
Coach R204 WYD

September 2nd 2004
Spinnaker Tower before
completion

## UK & Continental Touring

**Hellyers** of Fareham

| Company Background | Private Hire | UK & Continental Touring | Excursions & Holiday Programme | Contract Hire | Vehicle List | Maintenance Facilities |

**W**e are experienced in providing vehicles for either UK or Continental touring and we have visited and toured through most European countries.

Our fleet includes luxury executive vehicles which are equipped for this purpose.

In addition, we are able to provide our customers with hotel, ferry or shuttle booking facilities which enables us to tailor a tour to the specific requirements of customers.

*Coach Hire for all occasions*

September 7th 2004

View from 'Anker hotel', Brodenbach

Coach W2 HOF

September 2004, Brodenback, Germany to Ersk Castle


September 7th 2004

View from 'Anker hotel', Brodenbach

Coach W2 HOF

**Hellyers**

**of Fareham**

ort Fareham Business Park
Newgate Lane
Fareham
Hampshire
PO14 1AH

☏ 01329 285432
☏ 01329 235267

# Château du Tertre

**Itineraire**

Le Château

CHAUFFEUR

**AUTOCARS:  Hellyers**

## DOMFRONT - FRANCE

## 4 Day Tour

| JOUR | PETIT DEJ. | MATIN | DEJEUNER | APRES-MIDI | DINER | ACTIVITE DU SOIR |
|---|---|---|---|---|---|---|
| **LUNDI** 13 septembre 04 | | | | Bienvenue! 16h30 | 18h50 | Chasse aux informations |
| **MARDI** 14 septembre 04 | 7h50 | Activités Descente en rappel Parcours d'orientation Trapèze | Pique-nique | Goûter à la Ferme 14h30 St.-Georges-de-Rouell | 18h40 | Mini-Olympiades |
| **MERCREDI** 15 septembre 04 | 8h10 | Le Marché Gorron ou Flers | Pique-nique | Activités Canöe Descente en rappel Exercices d'Initiative | 18h00 | Soirée autour du feu |
| **JEUDI** 16 septembre 04 | 8h10 | Activités Canöe Trapèze Exercices d'Initiative | Pique-nique | Fougères Le Château | 18h40 | Soirée à l'auberge |
| **VENDREDI** 17 septembre 04 | 7h50 | A Bientôt! | Pique-nique | | | |

September 14th 2004. Staying at Ambrieries Chateau du Tertre, France
Coach T763 JYB

Visit to the butter making farm near Ambrieries

September 17th 2004 on return journey to St Malo
stopped at a supermarket

Old Fort and off-shore battle reamins

September 25th 2004

Historical group visits coastal battlefield remains

Coach A19 HOF

Omer Beach Landing area

Coastal ruins on battlefield beaches

The Landing beach map

Pegasus Bridge Cafe

Parachutist lands on the church

A memorial to the parachute soldier

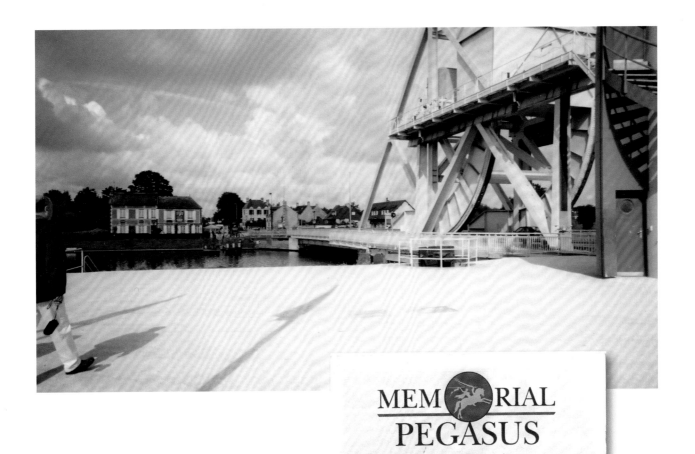

Pegasus Bridge

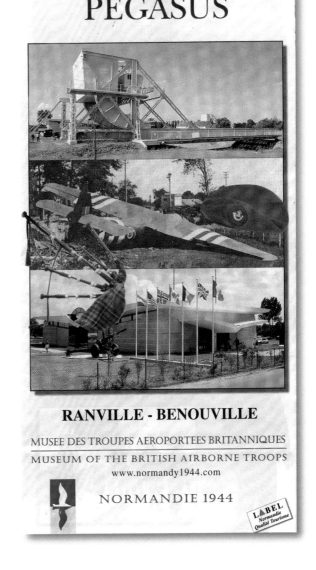

## Prato Nevoso Skiing Holidays

Resort Height: **1500m**

Prato Nevoso is a welcome new addition to
the Crystal programme and is an ideal
place to learn to ski or snowboard. Lying
on the north-west facing slopes of the
Maritime Alps the resort enjoys a good
snow record and plenty of sunshine.
Snowboarders are particularly well catered
for in the Board Park which has a half pipe
and is often illuminated in the evening too.
In fact, Prato Nevoso hosted the Junior
Snowboard World Championships in 2005. The two areas of Artesina and Prato
Nevoso make up the Mondole Ski area with almost 100kms of piste with many
gentle runs ideally suited to beginners and intermediates.

### Apres Sk:
An informal atmosphere with reasonably priced restaurants and bars
conveniently located opposite the slopes.

### Activities
• Snowpark • `Pratolandia` children`s snow playground • Ice skating • Ice
karting • Snow tubing • Night skiing

### Other Amenities
Shops • Cinema (Italian)

### Resort Statistics

- Highest Lift: **2092m**
- Km of Piste: **90km**
- Longest Run: **4km**
- Cross Country Trails: **n/a**
- Beginner Slopes: **23**
- Intermediate Slopes: **21**
- Advanced Slopes: **1**
- Mtn Restaurants: **14**
- Lifts: **23**
- Pass Photo Required:

### Suitability Guide

| | |
|---|---|
| Suitable for families: | X [No] |
| Suitability for beginners: | ●●●●●[5] |
| Suitability for intermediate skiers: | ●●●[3] |
| Suitability for advanced skiers: | ●●[2] |
| Suitability for boarders: | ●●●[3] |

January 6th 2005

Coach A19 HOF

Ski Tour Prato Nevoso, Italy

Go-kart track

Views from ski slopes

Waiting for ski-lift

Sun rise at Prato Nevoso

View of snow capped mountains

Lone Skier

Ski Slopes, Prato Nevoso

Coach X4 HOF

February 13th 2005. On way to La Polsa, Italy

Ski resort - Transport for the day.

February 19th 2005

Ready to leave La Polsa

Visit to Lake Garda (ferry)

March 2005 Visit to Calbourne Mill, Isle of Wight
Coach A18 HOF

March 19th 2005 Oakhampton, Devon. Bodmin Moor
Coach A18 HOF

PREVIOUS PICTURE    NEXT PICTURE

**View over Morzine**

## Ski Facts

| | |
|---|---|
| **Beginner** | ***** |
| **Intermediate** | ***** |
| **Advanced** | ***** |
| **Number of Runs** | 8  19 25  9 |
| **Height of Area** | 2400m |
| **Size of Area** | 130km |
| **Snowboarding** | Y |
| **Inclusive Lift Pass** | 6 day Morzine/Les Gets pass PLUS one day Portes du Soleil pass |
| **Lifts To** | 2400m |
| **Total Lifts** | 55 |
| **Longest Run** | 4.4km |
| **Ski Bus Included** | Yes |
| **Lift Pass Photo Required** | Yes |
| **Snow Cannon Coverage** | 40% |
| **Nearest Doctor** | Morzine |
| **Nearest Hospital** | Cluses/Thonon (30km) |

**Swimming:** Cluses
**Ice Skating:** Morzine
**Bowling:** Morzine

## Portes du Soleil - Morzine

The Portes du Soleil covers a huge expanse naturally separate skiing areas, encompassi Morzine, Les Gets and Avoriaz. PGL groups a accommodated in Morzine, an attractive and lively resort with extensive facilities for grou which hosted part of the Albertville Winter Olympics.

The PGL Lift pass covers all lifts in Morzine a Les Gets. The mainly north and north-west facing slopes provide excellent skiing conditi for beginners and intermediates along tree l runs. The Pleney plateau offers beginners a choice of runs, all leading back down to the village of Morzine. Intermediates will enjoy 1 red run down from the top of Les Chavanne: cable car. Included in your lift pass is one da skiing for the whole of the Portes du Soleil s area, providing excellent opportunities for th advanced skier. Between Champery and Avc only the very bravest skiers should attempt Wall' - an extreme black run which is almost impossible for all but the most experienced skier, maintaining an average gradient of 34 degrees.

## Chalet Les Flocons :: Morzine

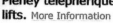

The Chalet is situated around 600 metres from the resort of Morzine centre and 800 metres from the Pleney téléphérique lifts. More Information about this hotel

## Standard Skiing courses for this hotel:

**Portes du Soleil - Chalet Les Flocons by coach :: 9days/8nights**

KEY

This area offers skiing above 2000m.

This accommodation offers doorstep skiing.

PGL can arrange snowboarding at any of our resorts.

Coach W2 HOF

March 25th 2005. Ski trip to Morzine, France.

A Chateau in Morzine

# Claviere

Accommodations in Claviere : Hotel Passero Pellegrino, Hotel

**Lovely old village with character but with doorstep skiing a convenience. Very high and snow sure with 2 free days on Way included on the pass. A new, high-speed 4 chair repla draglifts from the mid station at La Coche. This will be grea and snowboarders.**

Always one of our most popular destinations, this lovely little villa improve every year, and if you first got your ski legs here a few s have a surprise in store! As part of the Turin 2006 Olympic Game investment in the whole area. You'll find all the charm still intact I improvements to the village and the developing relationship with Montgenevre have propelled Claviere into a different league.

There's so many of the right ingredients in place here. The local s by delightful tree runs, is excellent, but your pass also includes 2 Milky Way, one of the biggest systems in the world. Our ski map I to the Claviere skiing because it's dwarfed by the Milky Way as a runs are varied and attractive, curving through trees on the shoul divide between Italy and France. Like neighbouring Montgenevre, first class. For beginners, there's a pleasant, flat area in the villag blue run which starts above the trees and goes all the way back t long and quite demanding, but enthusiastic beginners will feel a g achievement if they can manage all of it. Intermediates have mar some adventurous semi off-piste down little paths which wind thr seem to go on forever. Advanced skiers have some good reds, so piste, and there's the Milky Way to explore. It's a long day but a g out, last lift back!

You will certainly want to visit Montgenevre at least once. On the intermediates can enjoy one of the best runs on the Milky Way, fr dramatic Roc l'Aigle, down the wild and beautiful Colletto Verde, f colossal schuss home.

Claviere's height (1760m) and exposed position on the top of a pi exceptional snow security. Conditions are as good as anywhere in glacier resorts. Claviere has always been appreciated as a good v was actually one of Italy's first resorts. There's an attractive sens has masses of character and low priced border-town shopping. Or things about Claviere is the many traditional mountain restaurant reached by all levels of skier. We also recommend the first class s

We organise a lively après ski programme including a riotous skid mountain restaurant for an Italian banquet with lots of grolla! The and ice skating rink are also good fun. Montgenevre is a brisk 20r ride for a night out.

## book your holiday ▶ ▶ ▶

### resort facts

| beginners | 3 |
|---|---|
| intermediates | 5 |
| advanced | 4 |
| expert | 3 |
| non-skiers | 3 |
| apres ski | 3 |
| snowboarding | 4 |
| village height | 1760m |
| top lift | 2409m |
| marked runs | 50km/400km |
| snowmaking | yes |
| cable cars | -/1 |
| gondola | n/a |
| chair lifts | 6/27 |
| drag lifts | 8/38 |
| slopes | NE,NW |
| lift pass | Claviere and 2 free days on Italian Milky Way |
| photo needed | no |
| mtn restaurants | 3 |
| kindergardern | no |
| airport transfer | 1 1/2 hours |

### ski pack prices from

| 6 days lift pass | £71 |
|---|---|
| 6 days ski equip | £37 |
| Collective ski classes | £56 |
| Insurance | £35 |

### snow data

| date | 29/12/04 |
|---|---|
| resort depth | 40cm |
| conditions | Compact and Powder |
| mid stn depth | 40cm-60cm |
| conditions | Compact and Powder |
| top stn depth | 60cm |
| conditions | Compact and Powder |
| last snow fell | 28/12/04 |
| forecast | None forecast |
| pistes open | 11/12 (Claviere) |
| lifts open | 52 out of 62 (Milky Way) |
| beginners | Very good for beginners. |
| advanced | Good skiing conditions |

# Montgenèvre

## Montgenevre

Accommodations in Montgenevre : Chalet L'Ourson, Hotel Ro

**A convenient but natural ski area with a lovely old village. non-glacier conditions in France. Very high and snow sure local skiing and cheap links to the Milky Way.**

This is one of those rare resorts with everything! The attractive ol Montgenevre is convenient, snowsure and extensive with brilliant standards and with high mileage available for those who want it. I our hotel you can see a vast, white expanse of gently shelving slc Beyond is a wide bowl, mostly above the trees. Behind the hotel i facing side which you reach after a long schuss and short walk, or the village. It's less accessible, quieter, uncrowded and is a brillia morning blast.

The ski pass includes Claviere and Cesana which adds about 50% intermediates can ski there and back. There has been a lot of inve years, both in Montgenevre and neighbouring Claviere, and the cc more lifts, pistes and links every year. You can now ski sans front of the pass and the whole area is fully integrated. A new reservoir to supply the snowmaking system, which can now cover most of t Beginners have a great choice, not only on the superb village runs well. They can ski all the way home on an easy blue path to gain sense of achievement. The ski school is friendly and the instructor English.

Intermediates have plenty of choice, including sweeping blue runs moguls, some pretty tree runs and now, the fantastic Colletto Ver year, a fast four person chair replaced the uncompromising dog-le Rocher de l'Aigle. There are dramatic, craggy outcrops and great then a beautiful run, partially off-piste, all the way to Claviere.

Much of the Montgenevre terrain gets unofficially pisted by skiers gullies and trees between the pistes which almost doubles the offi Experts have three or four blacks and we also recommend the che to the Milky Way, giving over 400km of great skiing in all. Absolut are happy here.

Montgenevre village is a delightful jumble of old stone buildings c church. Unlike most French resorts it's an authentic mountain con established on the pass for centuries and with loads of character.

Montgenevre was France's first ski resort and you can see the ren lift next to the abandoned fortress overlooking the pass. Night life fairly lively, centred on a sprinkling of bars and the ice rink. The b one of the focal points.

## Village Facts

Traditional village on a high pass with a long skiing pedigree. Firs! in 1907. Convivial atmosphere. We are the biggest operator here.

## book your holiday

### resort facts

| beginners | 5 |
|---|---|
| intermediates | 4 |
| advanced | 3 |
| expert | 3 |
| non-skiers | 3 |
| apres ski | 3 |
| snowboarding | 4 |
| village height | 1850m |
| top lift | 2700m |
| marked runs | 100km/ Claviere 50km |
| snowmaking | Main runs to resort covered |
| cable cars | 1 |
| gondola | 2 |
| chair lifts | 10/5 |
| drag lifts | 14/7 |
| slopes | S,N,W |
| lift pass | Montgenevre, Claviere and Cesana |
| photo needed | No |
| mtn restaurants | 2/3 |
| kindergardern | Yes |
| airport transfer | 1.5 hours |

### ski pack prices from

| 6 days lift pass | £82 |
|---|---|
| 6 days ski equip | £37 |
| Collective ski classes | £68 |
| Insurance | £35 |

### snow data

| date | 29/12/04 |
|---|---|
| resort depth | 45cm |
| conditions | Snow is good down in resort |
| mid stn depth conditions | N/A |
| top stn depth | 70cm |
| conditions | High winds have caused some icy patches |
| last snow fell | 28/12/04 |
| forecast | 29/12/04 |
| pistes open | 50/81 |
| lifts open | 5/30 |
| beginners | Good and getting better everyday |
| advanced | Good and getting better everyday |

December 17th 2005 Ski holiday in Montgenerve
Coach HF03 HOF

Montgenerve, French Tunnel

December 21st. Parked at Ski resort

Montgenerve resort
December 21st, trip to Briancon

## Prato Nevoso Skiing Holidays

**Resort Height:1500m**

Prato Nevoso is a welcome new addition to the Crystal programme and is an ideal place to learn to ski or snowboard. Lying on the north-west facing slopes of the Maritime Alps the resort enjoys a good snow record and plenty of sunshine. Snowboarders are particularly well catered for in the Board Park which has a half pipe and is often illuminated in the evening too. In fact, Prato Nevoso hosted the Junior Snowboard World Championships in 2005. The two areas of Artesina and Prato Nevoso make up the Mondole Ski area with almost 100kms of piste with many gentle runs ideally suited to beginners and intermediates.

**Apres Sk:**
An informal atmosphere with reasonably priced restaurants and bars conveniently located opposite the slopes.

**Activities**
• Snowpark • `Pratolandia` children`s snow playground • Ice skating • Ice karting • Snow tubing • Night skiing

**Other Amenities**
Shops • Cinema (Italian)

**Resort Statistics**

- Highest Lift: **2092m**
- Km of Piste: **90km**
- Longest Run: **4km**
- Cross Country Trails: **n/a**
- Beginner Slopes: **23**
- Intermediate Slopes: **21**
- Advanced Slopes: **1**
- Mtn Restaurants: **14**
- Lifts: **23**
- Pass Photo Required:

**Suitability Guide**

Suitable for families:     x [No]

Suitability for beginners: ●●●●●[5]

Suitability for intermediate skiers:     ●●●[3]

Suitability for advanced skiers:     ●●[2]

Suitability for boarders:     ●●●[3]

# Prato Nevoso, Italy

Hotel Mondole.   Plenty of snow!

January 22nd 2006   Ski Trip
Coach A19 HOF

Good ski resort

Plenty of snow

January 27th

Another deep snow fall

# April 2nd 2006   La Plagne, French Alps

Coach A17 HOF

Belle Hotel

April 7th   Plenty of snow at ski resort

La Plagne ski lifts

April 27th 2006
Coach A3 HFU

MR ANTHONY COOKE
COACH DRIVER
HELLYERS
883 – 615 – 569

*21015339*

VISITOR

Commercial Vehicle Show
NEC Birmingham

# Excursions & Holiday Programme

**Hellyers of Fareham**

| Company Background | Private Hire | UK & Continental Touring | Excursions & Holiday Programme | Contract Hire | Vehicle List | Maintenance Facilities |

**O**ur comprehensive programme of excursions provides a wide range of day trips. We cater for all tastes by providing visits to many popular attractions; horticultural gardens, theme parks, historic buildings, markets, or simply scenic trips through the countryside. Our theatre programme provides our customers with the opportunity of seeing West End shows and is increasingly popular.

The excursion programme is co-ordinated through retail shops located in Gosport and Portsmouth.

These sales points are supplemented by a number of selling agents who have been appointed to provide convenient alternative booking points for our customers.

We operate an excursion club membership scheme for our customers that allows priority booking at discounted rates.

Our staff will be willing to assist with any enquiry for membership of this scheme.

*Coach Hire for all occasions*

⚬ Tour Programme   ⚬ Excursions   ⚬ Special Events

October 6th 2006

Shanklin Pier (remains) Isle of Wight

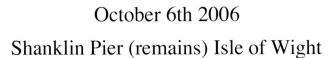

October 12th 2006

Coach YN51 MFZ

Milford on Sea clifftops (Views of Isle of Wight)

October 20th 2006 Day tour to Barton on Sea

Coach YN51 MFZ

October 15th 2006 Entering Eastleigh Airport, Southampton

# The Perranporth Hotel

36 St Pirans Road
Perranporth
TR6 0BJ
01872 573234
e-mail  perranporthhotel@btconnect.com
www.perranporthhotel.co.uk

## Bed & Breakfast Tariff 2006
(Prices per room per night)

| | 1st Jan to 14th July & 2nd Sept to 31st Dec | 15th July to 1st September |
|---|---|---|
| SINGLE | £30 | £40 |
| SINGLE OCCUPANCY OF DOUBLE/TWIN | £40 | £75 |
| DOUBLE/TWIN | £60 | £75 |
| TREBLE | £70 | £80 |
| FAMILY ROOM (Double with Bunks) | £75 | £90 |
| FAMILY ADJOINING (Double and twin room) | £90 | £110 |

Stays of 7-13 nights DEDUCT 10%
Stays of 14 nights or more DEDUCT 15%
Children under 3 in own travel cot are free of charge.
Additional camp-style beds are available at the additional rate of £5 per night (children only).

Bookings are confirmed with a £25 per person deposit either by credit/debit card at time of booking or by cheque within 7 days. The balance of accommodation charges are payable upon check-in at the Hotel.

We endeavour to have all rooms ready for arrival prior to 2pm on day of check-in and rooms are to be vacated by 10am on the day of departure.

## Special Offers 2006
All prices include Full English Breakfast

### 4 NIGHT BREAK
£90 PER PERSON
(£25.00 Children)
Available for bookings between
1st January – 20th May &
15th September – 19th December

### 3 NIGHT BREAK
£75 PER PERSON
(£15.00 Children)
Available for bookings between
1st January – 20th May &
15th September – 19th December

### 7 NIGHT SPECIAL
£165.00 PER PERSON
(£45 Children)
Available for bookings between
1st January – 15th July &
15th September – 16th December

Offers only available for advance bookings at least 7 days prior to arrival.
Children under 3 free
Age 3-12 - Child tariff
Over 12 – Adult tariff.

LIMITED AVAILABILITY
SO BOOK EARLY

Parked at Perranporth   316 service Y10 HOF

116

October 20th 2006 meeting at Hellyers. Bova Coach

Hellyers, Fort Fareham depot
Coaches Y14 HOF, 1AZ 4816, W664 KYB

Coaches TG04 HOF, KF05 HOF

Coaches PG04 HOF, TY62 JYB

Coaches AF03 HOF, GF05 HOF

Coaches BF03 HOF, UF04 HOF, M477 UYA

February 2007
Zenith Coach
CEZ 5292

Winter Ski Tour
to
Italy
for 7 days

**Prato Nevoso**
currently celebrating its
fortieth birthday, has
recognised asone of he
most resplendent and
beautiful truths offered by
winter tourism,throughout
the entire Italian alps.
You quickly learn how to
understand it and following
our helpful suggestions
fully embrace and enjoy it.
Whether it's a relaxed
and peaceful time you
are looking for or one
full ofaction, you will
not be disappointed.

February 16th 2007
Snow-capped
mountain view



Ideal place for children
to learn to ski and
snow board

## Prato Nevoso Skiing Holidays

**Resort Height: 1500m**

Prato Nevoso is a welcome new addition to the Crystal programme and is an ideal place to learn to ski or snowboard. Lying on the north-west facing slopes of the Maritime Alps the resort enjoys a good snow record and plenty of sunshine. Snowboarders are particularly well catered for in the Board Park which has a half pipe and is often illuminated in the evening too. In fact, Prato Nevoso hosted the Junior Snowboard World Championships in 2005. The two areas of Artesina and Prato Nevoso make up the Mondole Ski area with almost 100kms of piste with many gentle runs ideally suited to beginners and intermediates.

**Apres Ski:**
An informal atmosphere with reasonably priced restaurants and bars conveniently located opposite the slopes.

**Activities**
• Snowpark • 'Pratolandia' children's snow playground • Ice skating • Ice karting • Snow tubing • Night skiing

**Other Amenities**
Shops • Cinema (Italian)

**Resort Statistics**

- Highest Lift: 2092m
- Km of Piste: 90km
- Longest Run: 4km
- Cross Country Trails: n/a
- Beginner Slopes: 23
- Intermediate Slopes: 21
- Advanced Slopes: 1
- Mtn Restaurants: 14
- Lifts: 23
- Pass Photo Required:

**Suitability Guide**

| | |
|---|---|
| Suitable for families: | ✗ [No] |
| Suitability for beginners: | ●●●●● [5] |
| Suitability for intermediate skiers: | ●●● [3] |
| Suitability for advanced skiers: | ●● [2] |
| Suitability for boarders: | ● ● ● [3] |

Zenith coach and Mini bus base

HMS Daedalus, Lee-on-Solent

# ZENITH

## Tours and Excursions

**ZENITH** *At Lee On Solent* **TRAVEL**

**WINTER/SUMMER 2007**

| | | January | Adult | Senior | Child |
|---|---|---|---|---|---|
| Mon | 8th | Sailsbury Shopping 'New Year Sales' | £13.50 | £12.50 | £10.00 |
| Sat | 20th | Holiday on Ice, Brighton | £30.00 | £29.00 | £26.00 |
| Thurs | 25th | Holiday on Ice, Brighton | £30.00 | £29.00 | £26.00 |
| Sat | 27th | Legoland, Windsor | £30.00 | £27.00 | £25.00 |
| | | **February** | **Adult** | **Senior** | **Child** |
| TBC | TBC | Mystery Tour (inc: afternoon cream tea) | £12.50 | £12.50 | £10.00 |
| Sat | 10th | Chicago: Starring Jennifer Ellison | £35.00 | £33.00 | £30.00 |
| Tues | 13th | Swindon Designer Outlet Village | £10.00 | £10.00 | £10.00 |
| Tues | 27th | Beaulieu | £21.00 | £18.00 | £15.00 |
| | | **March** | **Adult** | **Senior** | **Child** |
| Fri | 9th | Black Country Living Museum | £25.00 | £23.00 | £21.00 |
| Sat-Thurs | 17th-22nd | 6 Day Break in IRELAND | £456.00 | £456.00 | £456.00 |
| Mon | 26th | Lakeside' shopping | £15.00 | £14.00 | £12.00 |
| TBC | TBC | Mystery Tour (inc: afternoon cream tea) | £12.50 | £12.50 | £10.00 |
| Fri | 30th | Marwell Zoo | £18.50 | £17.50 | £14.50 |
| | | **April (HALF TERM)** | **Adult** | **Senior** | **Child** |
| Tues | 2nd | Thorpe Park | £32.00 | £30.00 | £26.00 |
| Thurs | 4th | Marwell Zoo | £18.50 | £17.50 | £14.50 |
| Wed | 11th | Chessington World of Adventure | £32.00 | £30.00 | £30.00 |
| Thurs | 12th | Scooby Doo @ Mayflower | £28.00 | £26.00 | £23.00 |
| Tues | 17th | Bath Shopping Trip | £15.00 | £13.50 | £12.00 |
| | | **May** | **Adult** | **Senior** | **Child** |
| Thurs | 10th | Oxford | £10.00 | £10.00 | £10.00 |
| Sat | 19th | Highclere Castle | £18.00 | £16.00 | £14.00 |
| Mon | 28th | Sherbourne Castle Country Fair | £18.50 | £18.50 | £14.50 |
| TBC | TBC | Spring @ Exbury Gardens | £18.00 | £18.00 | £14.00 |
| | | **June** | **Adult** | **Senior** | **Child** |
| Mon -Sat | 1th-16th | 5 Nights/6 Days in 'Lake District' | £282.50 | £282.50 | £282.50 |
| Mon | 18th | Dirty Dancing Theatre Show | £50.00 | £50.00 | |
| Sun | 24th | Longleat Safari | £25.00 | £21.00 | £21.00 |
| Sun | 17th | Groombridge Place & Gardens (Pride & Prejudice) | £20.00 | £17.60 | £16.60 |
| | | **July** | **Adult** | **Senior** | **Child** |
| Mon - Fri | 23rd-27th | Disney Land & Trip in Paris | TBC | TBC | TBC |
| Sun | 22nd | Sherbourne Castle 'Classic Car Show' | TBC | TBC | TBC |
| Tues | 31st | Thorpe Park | £32.00 | £30.00 | £26.00 |

*More trips for May onwards will be added as the year goes on, please ring for details*
*Also please ring for our London and Mayflower Shows as these are on going throughout the year*

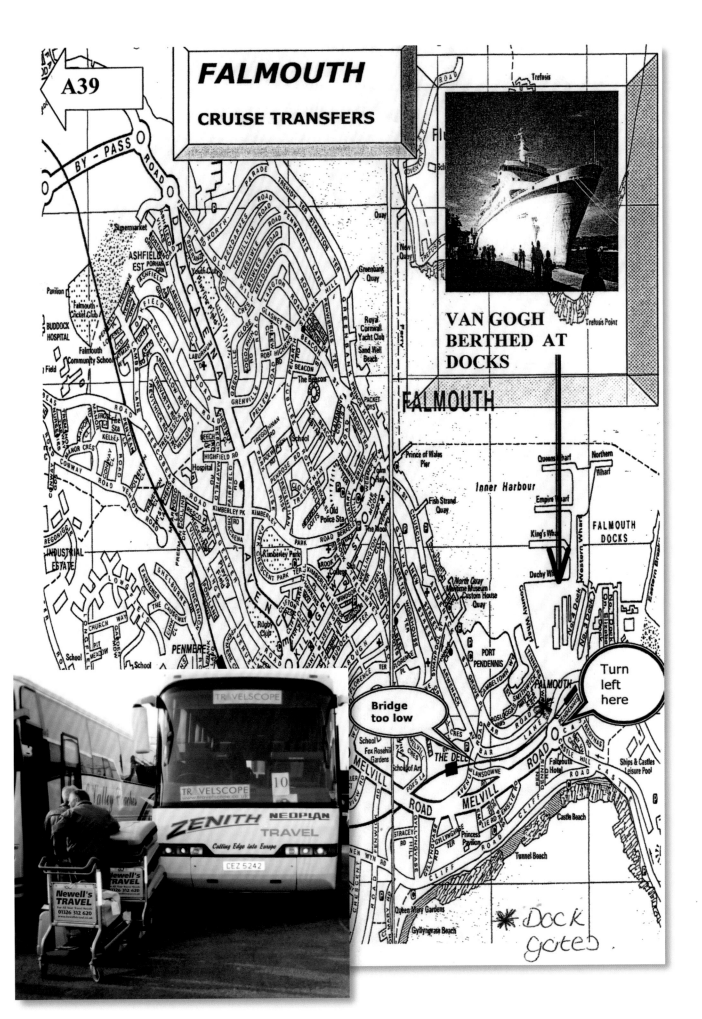

April 6th 2007 Falmouth Docks

Picking up passengers from the Van Gogh

Coach CEZ 5242

## DRIVERS INSTRUCTIONS

## OCEAN CRUISE TRANSFERS

### 06 APRIL 2007

### (RTW Inbound Coaching Only)

Travel empty to Falmouth Docks. Vehicles should be available from 08:30hrs.

Upon arrival in Falmouth make your way to the Docks (see enclosed map) Please do NOT go to the Maritime museum, directions will be given from dock gate. Once all passengers are on board return drop offs will commence.

Please be aware that these passengers have been aboard the Van Gogh for a three-month voyage. As such they are likely to be in possession of a large amount of luggage. Please ensure luggage compartments are cleared for use.

Please help us to help you by being co-operative to all Travelscope staff.

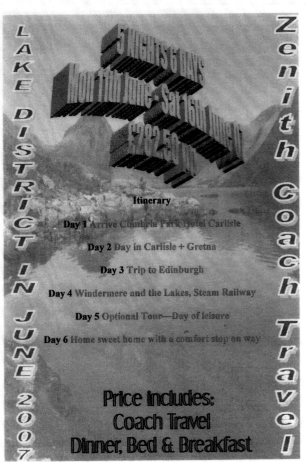

Excursion with Flyght Travel

Day out at the Eden Project

July 3rd 2008 Coach VIL 2915

Parked at Staunton Country Park

Staunton Park, overlooking the lake

# Battlefield Tours

Visit some of the most poignant
sights of the Ypres Salient and let
us take you back through history
on a moving journey that you
won't forget...

**October 3rd   2008**

**Brandhoek  Belgium, War Memorial. Passendale**

**Coach  P600 MPY**

October 3rd 2008 Coach P600 MPY

Brandhoek, Belgium   War Memorial, Passendale

# BATTLE FIELDS TOUR

**DAY 1**

Ypres ( leper area) via Hellfire corner & Menin Road.

Polygon Wood- counter attack by Worcester RGMT. Then on to Worcester memorial, drive on to Ypres and the Menin Gate.

The most famous commonwealth war memorial in Flanders.

20.00hrs Last post ceremony.

**DAY 2**

1. Sanctuary Wood  (Trenches & museums)

2. Hill 60 & Caterpillar Crater

3. Spanbroekmolen ( pool of peace view point)

4. New Zeland, memorial

5. Essex advanced dressing station + cemetery

6. Yorkshire trench

7. Langemark, German cemetery

8. Vancouver corner -Canadian memorial

# DAY 3

1. October 1917 Australian attack on foot from Zonnebeke

2. Tyne cottage + CWGC cemetery & memorial to the missing,   Passchendaele Ridge

3. Brandhoek . War cemetery

4. Poperinghe - death cell -firing post

Parked at Hill 60

# Battlefield Tours

## Command Bunker

| | |
|---|---|
| 1730 | Ferry Dover-Calais |
| By 2200 | ETA Hotels – time varies with hotel location. |
| **Day Two –** 0830 | **Day Two –** Depart hotel |
| 0930 | ETA Ypres (Ieper) area – via Hellfire Corner & Menin Road |
| 1000 | Stand 1 – Polygon Wood – Counter attack by 2nd Bn Worcestershire Regt. Then follow route of attack to Worcesters' Memorial |
| 1100 approx | Stand 2 - Visit German command bunker |
| 1130 | Stand 2 – Sanctuary Wood Preserved trenches & museum |
| 1430 | Stand 4 – Hill 60 |
| 1600 | Stand 5 – Essex Farm Advanced Dressing Station & CWGC Cemetery |
| 1700 | Stand 6 – Langemark German Cemetery (If time permits, visit Yorkshire Trench en route) |
| 1815-1930 | Meal in local restaurant - Ypres |
| 1930 | Stand 7 – Menin Gate |
| 2000 | Last Post Ceremony |
| 2030 | Depart for Hotel |
| 2115 approx | Arrive Hotel |
| **Day Three** 0730 | **Day Three** Breakfast |
| 0915 | Stand 8 – Vancouver Corner - Canadian Memorial |
| 0945 | Stand 9 -Tyne Cot CWGC Cemetery & Memorial to the Missing – Passchendaele Ridge |
| 1100 | Stand 10 - Crest Farm |
| 1230 | Stand 11 – Visit Poperinghe a. Death cell b. Firing Post |
| 1330 | Depart Poperinghe for Calais |
| 1630 approx | Ferry Calais/Dover |

## Canadian Memorial

Brandhoek

Military Cemetary

Hill 60

Railway cutting

London Tour
October 10th 2007
Beatrice (the duck)

London Eye
Popular attraction

October 26th 2007
Kingston-on-Thames
Street scene

Coach used for local rowing club parked at Richmond-on-Thames

**The local team rowed from London to Paris via Ramsgate, Dover, Cap Gris Nez to Le Havre and up the Seine via Rouen to Paris; 417 nautical miles**

September 13th 2008. Cutters rowing Club, Langstone, Havant
Preparing to race

# 4 NIGHT/5 DAY TRIP
# TO THE
# ISLE OF WIGHT – 13/17 OCTOBER 2008

# ITINERARY.

## MONDAY 13 OCTOBER

After our local pickups we head for our ferry to cross to the Isle of Wight at approx 11.00a.m.
Once over the Isle of Wight we continue our journey with a stop at the Busy Bees centre for a stroll around and perhaps have a cup of tea with cake or pastry in the Honey Pot coffee shop.

The first stage of development of Busy Bee was just completed when the Great Storm of 1987 virtually flattened it. At the time the enterprise was no more than one small glasshouse and a couple of poly tunnels, the latter being completely destroyed. Busy Bee originated really by chance, the land on which it stands being bought purely as a pasture in which to keep a horse or two! However, when the present proprietors, Chris and Mary Leslie were having a picnic in the new field with their children the idea of a Garden Centre was first envisaged. Since that time, there has only been one aim, to be one of the best Garden Centres in the country. To this end quality has always been the prime criteria along with great depth of range of products stocked all at affordable prices. Busy Bees pride themselves in being different, offering plants and other products beyond the run of the mill items stocked by many other Garden Centres.

At approx 1500hours we continue our journey to our hotel, The Burlington. Once there we then have time to unpack and relax, perhaps enjoy the indoor pool, spa and steam room, before evening meal. Following our evening dinner entertainment will be in held the bar lounge.

## TUESDAY 14 OCTOBER:

Breakfast will be served between 08:15 and 09:15a.m. Today we board the coach (at approx 10:30) for a scenic trip to Arreton Barns.

Arreton Barns is a working craft village with glass blowing, ceramics and woodcrafts. There are a range of metal and craft shops including the Corn Exchange, Lavender & Lace and the Brewery Shop. An on-site brewery supplies ale to the pub - The Dairyman's Daughter. This is complemented by the tearoom. There is also a collection of agricultural memorabilia. We leave Arreton Barns at approx 14:00hours and head back to our hotel in time for relaxation or a seafront stroll before our evening meal, followed by evening entertainment in the bar lounge.

Day trip Coach V1L 9765

Weald & Downland Museum, Singleton, West Sussex

# Glorious Goodwood

Coach V1L 8671

Grandstand and Race Course

August 1st 2009   Another day at Glorious Goodwood

Goodwoood House, home of the Festival of Speed

Goodwood Motor Revival

Goodwooood Revival fly past and helicopter flights

144

# PLAY
# UP
# POMPEY

Kennet Valley, Newbury
Horse Drawn barge
September 19th 2009

DRIVER

# 23-27 DECEMBER 2009
# 4 NGHT/5 DAY
# CHRISTMAS BREAK

This beautiful Grade II listed Country House Hotel is set admist 11 acres of landscaped gardens and parkland, approximately 3 miles from Coventry City Centre.  The original Manor House, built in 1894 by the car manufacturer William Hillman, has been tastefully extended over the years to become the largest hotel in Coventry.

This stunning Coventry countryside hotel offers 210 en-suite bedrooms in a peaceful and tranquil setting.  All rooms are traditionally decorated and include TV, Telephone, Trouser Press, Hairdryer and Tea & Coffee making facilities. Some have views overlooking the Coventry Countryside.

The Royal Court Hotel in Coventry offers extensive facilities to suit both the business and leisure guest.  The Carvery Restaurant is situated in the Baronial Hall making this a popular hotel in Coventry with the locals and visitors alike.  Adjacent the Balmoral Bar offers a cosy enviroment to relax overlooking the grounds.

The Spindles Health Club at the Royal Court Hotel is equipped with an 18m indoor heated swimming pool, sauna, steam room, Spa, Hair & Beauty Salon and Large multi purpose Gym.  Access is charged at £5.00 per person for hotel guests for the duration of your stay.

BED/FULL ENGLISH BREAKFAST & EVENING MEAL

WITH LOTS OF ENTERTAINMENT

VISIT FROM SANTA TO INCLUDE A PRESENT

COACH INCLUDING ALL THE ABOVE

£299.00 PER PERSON

**(Single supplement of £25 per stay)**

Welcome to
The Anglican Shrine of
Our Lady of Walsingham

July 17th 2010
Coach P70 SEL
Walsingham, Norfolk

Light Minature
Railway,
Walsingham to
Wells, next the sea

Coach line up, Bedhampton, 2009

Snow fall, Bedhampton, 2010

Vision Coaches & Mini Buses, Lee-on-Solent, 2011

# ZENITH DRIVER TRAINING

**ZENITH**
DRIVER TRAINING

THIS IS  CERTIFY THAT

# Anthony Cooke

## Has successfully completed Basic Assessment

Vehicle Lift Training.
Including the safe use of Fitted Vehicle Lifts .

Course Date:   03/03/11          End Date:   03/03/12

Instructor:   Richard McKeown   ITSSAR: 1:14494

Signature:

Certificate No:      WCA030312-rm-1

Address: Hanger D 289 HMS Daedalus Lee-On-Solent  PO13 9YA

Authorized By: D.SHARPE (Director)      ITSSAR: 2:10265

This training conforms to the requirements of Health and Safety Commission Approved Code of Practice and
Guidance rider operated lift trucks operator training.

# Popular Excursions and Tours

## from the Portsmouth area

Adinkerke (city europe )

Arundel carpet of flowers

Amberley museum

Bath market

Beaulieu motor museum

Bird world & Garden Centre

Bournemouth

Bognor Regis

Brighton sea front & ice shows

Blue water & lakeside shopping

Blue Bell Line

Covent Garden & Transport museum

Christchurch market & shops

Chelsea Flower show

Chelsea Barracks

Camden Lock & Pettiecoat Lane

Cheddar Gorge & Caves

Cotswold

Chichester Canal

Canterbury

Lymington market

Lyme Regis

Longleat Safari Park

Legoland

Littlehampton

Monkey World (Dorset)

Marwell Zoo

Olde Tyme Players

Paultons Park

Portsmouth Gun Wharf

Petworth House/

Jane Austins &

Gilberts House

Poole Pottery·

Ringwood

Salisbury Cathedral

Sidmouth sea front

Swanage

Southampton Shows

Stitch & Craft Shows

| | |
|---|---|
| Eastbourne sea front | Thorpe Park |
| Exbury Gradens | War Museum |
| Fishbourne Roman Palace | Winchester market |
| Goodwood Horse Races | Weymouth sea front |
| Goodwood Festval Speed & Revival | Wimbourne market |
| Hampton Court & Kew Gardens | Wisley Gardens |
| Ideal Home Exhibition | Worthing |
| Isle of Wight Tours | Weald & Downland |
| Kennet Valley Horse Drawn Barge | Museum |
| London Theatres/shops & tours | |

Barry McGuire (Trippin' the Sixties)
visits from the United States
May 2009

# THURSDAY 28 AUGUST 2008
# GREAT DORSET STEAM FAIR

The Great Dorset Steam Fair is widely recognised as the World's leading steam and vintage vehicle preservation event and is attended every year by over 200,000 people from the U.K and from all over the World!

You can see all of our features detailed on this site and keep track of days to go, check trade stand prices, information on exhibiting, see details of tickets for visitors, costs, advanced booking incentives, parking, camping and entertainments amongst other valuable information, plus the widely used chat and Q&A forums.

The show has something for everyone, whatever your interests! Maybe you are a collector, a steam fanatic, an exhibitor, a heavy horse fan, an avid camper, a music fan or just on holiday in the south of England at the end of August and fancy an excursion to what is described as the most remarkable show on earth!

2008 sees the Great Dorset Steam Fair in its 40th year

# COACH & ENTRY TICKET

# ADULT £29.00/SENIOR £28.00

# CHILD £23.00

154